D1432308

Picture Yourself & the Life You Want

Picture Yourself & the Life You Want

A Proven Approach to Selling
from One of America's Leading Corporate Coaches
Leslie Groene

Co-Author
Tom Mills

Includes
100 Focus Points for Success

 **Tiger Publications**LLC

Published by
Tiger Publishing, LLC
Olympic Plaza Building
11500 Olympic Blvd., Suite 400
Los Angeles, CA 90064

Printed in the United States of America
Jacket Design by Michael Gallanes
Photos by Gary Mann

0-9753177-0-9

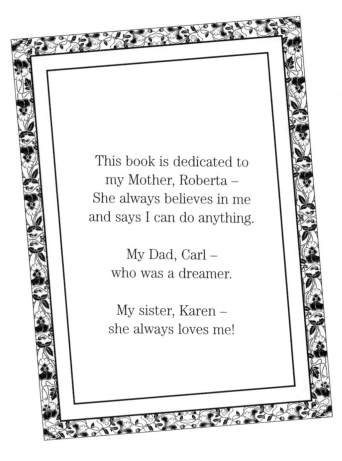

This book is dedicated to
my Mother, Roberta –
She always believes in me
and says I can do anything.

My Dad, Carl –
who was a dreamer.

My sister, Karen –
she always loves me!

Acknowledgements

I am grateful to:

- Bud Gottesman and Darryl LaFayette for giving me a chance to become a sales rep and many years later for having the faith in me that inspired me to become a sales consultant which lead to the creation of Groene Consulting.

- Randy Ginsberg for challenging me to become a more comprehensive, relationship driven sales professional.

- Dave Melin and Gary Tee for taking a chance that I could effectively lead a sales team.

- Larry Luchtel for being my first Groene Consulting client.

- Arleen Zavala and Jane Alonzi for asking me to be their sales coach which helped me transition my business into a more comprehensive customized company.

- The PIA Sales Club Board for putting up with me all these years.

- All my coaching clients throughout the years that have trusted me with their weaknesses and allowed me to push them past their comfort zones.

- Sandy Sedberry for being an excellent set of eyes and Dan Engler for providing top notch editorial assistance.

- Johnny Davila for his friendship and helping me pull off the production of the book.

- Michael Gallanes for the design, layout and creative input on the book.

- The Tuesday networking group for keeping me accountable and Jane Wick for keeping me sane.

- Gary Mann for his support, creativity and most of all, his patience

Contents

Picture Yourself
& the Life
You Want

"Just one more time...just one more time...just one more time." Those were the words I remember hearing so often from my coach during my years in gymnastics. As I look back, I don't think I ever heard him say, "Last time." In other words, "Keep going until you get it right." I remember wishing for an easier way to develop my skills, but, in the end I always found there was no substitute for the tried and true methods of the champions who had gone before me. Athletes in all sports are constantly looking for the latest, greatest and fastest way to get to the top. Sadly, you don't have to look too far to find stories of those who looked too hard for short cuts. Some athletes have become so desperate to succeed that they are even willing to compromise their integrity and their health through the use of performance-enhancing drugs.

In today's competitive business environment, we can also see an emphasis on the "latest and greatest" technological device or that hot "breakthrough" theory that is supposed to increase our productivity overnight. Certainly, such new devices and approaches appeal to us because we all want that edge that can help us to succeed throughout our careers. But we can also rely on some time-tested basics for that edge.

In *Picture Yourself & the Life You Want,* Leslie Groene and Tom Mills have provided this edge to you. After reading just a few pages, you will want to strive for excellence and you will buy in to this journey. Both Leslie and Tom have had a rather unique opportunity in their lives to know and observe some very successful individuals. As a result, this book is able to deliver proven approaches and concepts that have worked for both outstanding sales professionals and Olympic champions.

I have known Tom for more than 20 years. I met him when I was just another Olympic hopeful attempting to make the USA Gymnastics Team for the 1984 Los Angeles Olympic Games. His firm handled the marketing for the Southern California Olympians' ("SCO") alumni organization. As a result of his efforts, the SCO became the model for all other Olympian alumni organizations. Tom has a passion for the Olympic movement and has become a friend to many of the greatest Olympic athletes of all time.

We all will be hearing quite a lot about Leslie Groene in the future. Quite simply, like all effective coaches in life (and I've had great ones), she thrives on getting the best from her clients. In this book, both Tom and Leslie will help you to roll up your sleeves and earn the successful business and personal results that you deserve.

The authors also suggest many ways for you to unlock your own inner resources so that the work becomes something you enjoy in a balanced setting. After all, this is the important challenge most of us face in our lives. No one else can do your work for you. During those honest moments when we look in the mirror, we know how we're really doing in our pursuit of the life that we really want.

Remember, it is up to you to apply this guide. Leslie and Tom bring a collective 40-plus years of experience in sales and coaching-related endeavors to this project and their cut-to-the-chase style makes this book easy to read. May you find the keys you are looking for within this book so that the rest of your life may be a "Perfect 10."

Peter Vidmar
Olympic Gymnastics Champion, 1984
Author of *Risk, Originality & Virtuosity, the Keys to a Perfect 10*

Picture Yourself & the Life You Want

The Authors

This book is an exciting collaboration between Ms. Leslie Groene, a highly successful corporate coach, and Tom Mills, a veteran music production and sports marketing executive. Both are based in Southern California.

After graduating from Cal State University at Fullerton, Leslie Groene went to work for Zellerbach Paper in Los Angeles as a sales representative. After five years, she joined Penn Litho in a similar capacity. In 1988, she became a sales representative for George Rice & Sons, where she earned "Rookie of the Year" honors and became one of the company's leading producers.

In 1995, Leslie made the transition to sales management with Direct Color in Long Beach. In two short years, sales increased 50 percent. Groene was convinced that she was ready and able to establish Groene Consulting, which she did in 1997. Since that beginning, Groene Consulting has dramatically increased its sales – and just as importantly, its clients' sales have increased as well.

Today, Groene's clients include Fortune 500 companies, such as KPMG, Deloitte Consulting, Guest Supply, Inc. (a SYSCO company), the Capital Group and MeadWestvaco as well as major printing companies, medium and smaller-sized print firm owners, leading sales managers and sales representatives. As a result of her firsthand experience, Leslie has been able to provide valuable sales training seminars to many industries and groups such as the Advertising Production Club of Los Angeles, the Printing Industry Association, distribution sales companies, accounting management teams, real estate and financial professionals.

Tom Mills is a 1980 graduate of Loyola Law School. He has served as the founding partner of Track Record Enterprises LLC since 1979. Since its creation, his sports marketing and music production firm has worked with some of the leading companies and organizations in the U.S.A. including the University of Notre Dame, the 1984 Los Angeles Olympic Organizing Committee, the Southern California Olympians, Nike, Anheuser-Busch, Pepsi, Coca-Cola, AT&T and ABC Television.

In addition, Mills has worked with a number of high profile Olympian and entertainment celebrities and has been involved in marketing and media programs since the formation of his firm 25 years ago. He has worked with virtually all of the major electronic and print media and has executed marketing campaigns for both his music and sports divisions.

Picture Yourself
& the Life
& You Want

Introduction

We decided on the title for this book in our initial work session. We want to present a central theme that is both practical and compelling. Immediately, we realized that together we have 40-plus years of pursuing excellence in accomplishing individual and shared objectives. The title *Picture Yourself & the Life You Want!* is such a simple yet perfect fit for what you can achieve with this inspirational book.

All of us strive to "be the best we can be" in our daily lives. We all face countless obstacles, and we all allow ourselves from time to time to be sidetracked, either by the actions or inaction of others we depend upon or by our own counter-productive behavior. We want this book to provide you with practical guidelines you can use to significantly improve your performance in many areas of your life, so you can attain the excellence you seek and you can craft the life you want to have.

We will use many of the coaching techniques that Leslie employs in her coaching practice, as well as hypothetical examples of problems and solutions.

You will see that we have included a wealth of practical tips and examples that we have gleaned from our personal and collective experiences and observations. There will be examples of our "focus points" and some suggested items for your own "wish list." Attention to detail is a hallmark of this guidebook for personal and professional success. We believe in starting from the ground up and leaving no stone unturned (how's that for using a few cliches along the way?). So please take your time with the preliminary material. We all tend to get a little lax at times, and this refresher on the fundamentals will be useful reference material for you.

In addition, Tom will employ some analogies from his personal experience in the sports and entertainment industries. He will provide some specific examples of techniques that have enhanced both process and outcome in his life.

We wish to thank everyone who has assisted us over the years by their example (whether intentionally or unintentionally) and by their actions (or inaction). Like everyone, we sometimes also learn what not to do from those around us who fail to attain the results they desire. It is possible to learn from those whom we choose not to emulate.

Now, we invite you to read on so you can spend some time in meaningful reflection about where your life is and where you would like it to be. Consider the changes that you will need to make and what the cost will be in terms of time, energies and resources. We salute you for having the courage to commit to "being the person you can become." Here's to you, as you truly become the person you want to be!

"Daring
to
Dream"

At some point in our childhood, most of us are deeply affected by a role model who inspires us. This can be a parent, a brother, a sister or another relative. However, often it is someone who comes into our lives through a compelling sports event, television series, motion picture, music CD or DVD, or other entertainment form.

My co-author Tom's earliest powerful recollections involve both the stirring football tradition of the Fighting Irish of Notre Dame and the Olympic feats of Bob Mathias, the decathlon champion. Tom says the film "The Bob Mathias Story," starring Bob Mathias himself, inspired him to make an inner commitment to become an athlete – and he kept that commitment all the way through college.

My earliest role model was someone extremely close: my Mother, Roberta. I saw how devoted she was to her work and her clients. When she came home excited from closing a printing deal, I got excited and I just knew my destiny would involve working with clients in a sales capacity.

Unfortunately, many of us often lose touch with our dreams. Instead of receiving encouragement from those close to us, we become discouraged. Our parents might have been deeply affected by a family trauma when they were growing up, such as a bankruptcy that would become a source of shame for the entire family.

Avoiding shame was a powerful motivator for Americans in the World War II generation. Men experienced tremendous peer pressure to marry and to get a dependable, stable job. The war had taken a great toll, and people were driven to get on with their lives and find stability. Back then, some people considered entrepreneurs a little odd, although those who achieved great success were rewarded with adulation. Many families were first- or second-generation immigrants from Europe or Asia. Many of their sons and daughters became products of their new culture and sought to assimilate into American society.

Women also experienced a considerable amount of societal pressure to "find a man" and start a family. Many career ambitions were not "in the cards" for young females. They were encouraged to either stay at home to raise their families or to opt for careers in nursing and teaching or as secretaries or other supporting roles.

For whatever reason, many individuals who start with a dream decide not to pursue it. However, my primary focus in my work is with those who still believe in the power of a dream in shaping their goals and life plan. They understand that it is important to enjoy what they do to earn their living. Often, their enjoyment results from the special talents and abilities they use in their profession.

Right here, my co-author Tom wants to insert a sports metaphor to reinforce this point. He asks you to imagine yourself as the coach of a highly disciplined and talented college football team whose strengths are a tremendous offensive line and an All-American running back who specializes in powerful runs from behind that line. If this team succeeds in reaching the mythical national championship game, Tom would advise you as coach to do what you did to get to this point in the first place. Too often, individuals and companies seem to forget what they do best. In the hope of surprising their competitors, they deviate from their natural strengths and ultimately fail because of that.

I will ask you to think of the example of a young woman who enjoys expressing herself. At every opportunity, she passionately states her positions and tactfully influences listeners to her point of view. Obviously, because of her communication and argumentation skills, she should find an employment position that takes advantage of her gifts.

However, if she enters an environment that discourages these gifts, she will find herself dealing with increased stress and a tremendous decrease in the psychic benefits that she derives from her work. Hopefully, she will find another opportunity – either via promotion or in a related field – where she "can go to her strength" and she can use the precious gifts and talents that come so naturally to her.

We need dreams, but we also need to have the practicality that will make them happen. For instance, many of our dreams relate to basic considerations, such as losing weight for better health, short-term and long-term.

When someone loses a lot of weight, many added benefits kick in. First, by committing to a healthier process, the individual changes the type of food he or she eats regularly. Next, the person often makes a commitment to eat smaller portions of the healthful food. Most successful and lasting weight loss programs today include exercise components. After a brief period of regular exercise, a person will begin to feel better and stronger. Obviously, after someone loses a substantial amount of weight, those around him or her will notice the improved fitness and physical appearance, and this may contribute to a sense of enhanced self-worth.

When someone makes a commitment (I like to call it "buying in") and follows through consistently, their performance triggers a renewed sense of power in their life. When dealing with this performance – and I will say more about it later – I like to include four key components to assist my clients in their "buy-in."

First, I ask them to consider the concept of *momentum*. When we actually do what we say or commit to doing, we create a sense of momentum in our lives. For example, the first couple of times we add exercise to our lives, such as walking, jogging or working out at a health club or gym, we might experience some temporary soreness in muscles and joints as a result of this exertion. But if we continue the regular workout program, the temporary soreness goes away and we begin to train our muscles and improve our cardiovascular conditioning so that our exercising actually gets easier!

However, if we don't continue the exercise program, we lose that potential for momentum – and each time we do attempt to exercise again, after weeks have slipped by, we feel a little bit "behind the eight ball" because we don't have the increasing benefits of our successful performances to build upon.

As a result, my second key element plays a vital role in our attaining the dream we have. This element is *consistency*. Consistency is one of the most important elements in every aspect of our lives. It is vital for any authority figure who deals with children to be consistent with rules and communication patterns in the school and home. Consistency is also vital in the workplace as well. How many problems are created by an individual's failure to deliver what is expected of him or her in a given crucial situation?

For instance, if you are a sales associate who is depending upon the actions of a senior executive for a bid to be submitted and delays occur, you know what will happen to you if that executive drops the ball. Not only will you lose your potential commission, you might also have blown your chance with that client. When this happens, we feel as if we have been betrayed because often it takes all that we can do just to get that call for an estimate, bid or demo. And after all of the hard work that has been invested in getting that account, we know we deserve to be supported by our management team.

The third key element is the ability to be *patient*. This concept sounds simple, but how many of us can actually remain patient in the face of approaching deadlines and other day-to-day pressures? All commuters notice that this virtue is in short supply on their daily car trips to the office. Often, the craving for immediate gratification overcomes people's best efforts to be patient. However, the type of patience that we are preaching in this book is first an inner patience.

When we are applying our plans and seeking the results of those plans, we need to maintain our composure and be patient with ourselves! As all of us know, there will be times when we fall short and we don't get to the gym three times a week. We need to be able to maintain our focus and patiently get back to adhering to our plan. Don't immediately lose interest or fall back into negative behavior patterns (overeating or taking in the junk food).

When we experience our temporary setbacks and breaks in the momentum and consistency that we have enjoyed, we need to take a step back and again commit (patiently) to buying into the plan that we have established. For example, if we go three or four days without getting a workout in, we should just take the time to make that workout a top priority again. Nothing is more inspirational and satisfying than knowing you have encountered some adversity and overcome it!

This leads to the fourth element, which is *perseverance*. I like to define my corporate coaching work as "the ability to facilitate success in other people." This success results when my clients embrace the concept of accountability and take personal responsibility for the amount of success, or the lack of it, in their professional and personal lives. When I begin a new relationship with a coaching client, I attempt to convey the importance of this element early on.

I believe it is critical to my client's success for him or her to truly grasp the importance of finishing each and every important task each and every day. One device that I will discuss later in this book is the daily time and task log that I encourage my clients to keep. This valuable tool will enable my clients to truly gauge the amount of time that is allocated to specific tasks and clients and the returns that are realized. As a result, my clients can gain a vital perspective on where their time is being maximized and where it is being wasted or minimized.

It is very encouraging for me (and my motivation is also important in the client/coach equation) when I note that a new client is a long distance runner or has been involved in a specific hobby or interest for a substantial period of time. Sometimes, my clients reveal an earlier instance when they have overcome adversity or setbacks to attain a long-term goal or objective. I am encouraged because I know that this client will readily relate to the value of perseverance and embrace the sacrifices that are required to attain the desired outcome.

About now, you're probably thinking, "Leslie is spending a lot of time on this particular element." You're absolutely correct, because perseverance is one of those characteristics that leads to the development of a strong character in an individual. I like to tell my clients they should be thankful that they have had to overcome adverse circumstances. They have developed willpower, discipline and dedication as a result of being challenged.

In addition to these four key elements, I also am a strong advocate of maintaining *balance* in our lives. I believe in developing the "whole person." I recognize the need for growth in all of the human dimensions – professional, physical, spiritual and social. I believe that if one of these areas is out of balance and growth is not forthcoming, all of the other dimensions might be adversely affected.

How many times have we encountered an individual who possesses many of the "merit badges" of our corporate culture – the expensive car, the Italian designer wardrobe, the prestige home or apartment – only to discover an apparent major insecurity or character flaw that prevents this individual from attaining true success and contentment?

For example, someone might be extremely successful in a career but might also carry emotional baggage, have impaired ability to communicate, or struggle with weight gain, a lack of self-esteem or a crisis of faith. I believe that in such instances this person must deal with these problems because failures in those important dimensions will have consequences. Perhaps the person will seek to escape by drinking to excess or find other negative ways to sabotage his or her career success.

After all, how often have we seen marriages that seemed happy and content on the surface suddenly dissolve? Obviously, the couple was not effectively addressing certain things. I believe we must seek balance in every area of life. Therefore, my faith is extremely important to me. I don't wear it on my sleeve, but it is an important source of strength and rejuvenation for me when my batteries need recharging.

Additionally, for years I have maintained a consistent workout program through aerobic workouts. Actually, I am a certified instructor and I teach regular aerobics classes in a local fitness club. When I am a little stressed out, there is no better release for me than a rigorous session at my health club and I really enjoy the interaction with my fellow fitness enthusiasts.

Along with making time for the spiritual and the physical, I maintain a full professional business calendar of meeting with business owners, sales managers and sales associates. I find that keeping a busy and organized schedule keeps me on my toes and keeps me in "the know" with all of my clients. I also really enjoy just keeping up to date with my clients and associates on a regular basis, because I also think of them as my friends.

Finally, although my days are often extremely busy attending to the needs of my clients and business associates, I find the time to spend with family and my close friends. My family and friends have been there for me over the years and the time that I spend with these cherished loved ones refreshes me for all the work I must do.

Now that we have considered some of the key elements that need to be there to make our dreams actually come true (momentum, consistency, patience, perseverance and balance), let's begin to focus on our dream.

What do we want in our lives?

This seems so simple. But in our busy and fast-paced lives so many different messages are constantly competing for our attention. In this frenetic environment it is a challenge to find the time and focus to rediscover what we really desire in our lives. Obviously, there is a simple way to begin. All of us could use a little more compensation in our lives. Funny how many of the clients that I coach seem to always begin with the dream of financial independence.

Many of the beginners start with the dream of financial solvency. These young college grads have loans to pay off and new apartments to rent. They need to find a means just to get by initially so they won't have to end up moving back in with Mom and Dad!

However, for many of us money is just part of the picture. My clients crave more than just an increase in their incomes. They desire the respect and the freedom that comes with the success. For one of my clients, whom you will read about later, it all started with her desire for a new kitchen! That was enough to get her started.

Another of my clients just desired more quality time for himself and his family.

In my coaching sessions I believe in spending the time that is required to hone in on the true desires of my clients. Fortunately, I'm not someone who will judge them or divulge their secrets. I'm there to help them make it happen in the most direct and forceful manner possible.

Take a moment and just close your eyes and reflect about your dream. Was there a time in your youth that someone touched a chord deep inside of you and you thought, "I'd love to be like that person!" Maybe your first thought was, "I can do that!"

So just take a brief time out for a few minutes and think about the people and role models who influenced you when you were growing up. Think about the types of things you used to love to do. Think about any of the special gifts you have. Think about the causes that were or are close to your heart. Is there any one thing that beckons you like a beacon in the night?

Some of us still have something that we never quite completed and it is still in our minds even today. Some clients have expressed desires to me that had little to do with their professional careers, at least on the surface. However, as soon as they articulated the dream or objective, they acquired a newfound spirit and confidence that benefited their careers.

I am going to suggest a little assignment for you. Take some time and begin to think about your life today and previously. Take a brief inventory and go back in time in an attempt to rediscover your own passion or special gift. As I have explained, it could really be anything – work-related or not.

Once you find some answers, please ask yourself some additional questions. Are you using this special gift or talent in what you do today? Could you acquire your objective if you really made the time and commitment? What would be the benefit to you? Can you incorporate your gift, such as writing, in your current job? If your special talent or skill involves creativity, can you translate it into work-related benefits?

This is just food for thought. I believe that most of us do have our own unique gifts to give to our communities and our world. However, we must believe in those gifts and ultimately use those gifts to truly make a difference. For example, one of Tom's special talents is writing. When he was working his way through evening law school by selling real estate, he found a clever way to utilize this gift that made his job more rewarding and, ultimately, more profitable.

Because he was selling real estate in his hometown, he decided to create a newsletter that dealt with real estate considerations but also included a major section on his fellow high school classmates and their current lives. As a result, when he did his traditional prospecting (cold calls) to their parents who were still in the community, he would open the conversation by revealing that he was a classmate of "Susan or Bill" and he would ask the proud parents for updates on their children for publication in his local newsletter.

Quickly, the alumni section became the most popular section of his newsletter and led to a number of listings and sales and to enhanced relationships with those proud parents. Tom also was able to sell some of those former classmates homes in the community as well. And best of all, this creative approach transformed those chores of cold calling and farming into tasks that were easier to perform on a regular basis and more enjoyable and fulfilling for Tom and his newsletter readers.

Now, let's review what we have addressed in this opening chapter.

We have talked about the importance of role models in our lives. Consciously or unconsciously, most of us have been influenced by someone we admire. But many of us get discouraged by life experience, family or friends from really going after our dreams. Perhaps that's why we admire people who find success and true passion in their lives.

So our first key should be to listen to our hearts and to attempt to discover what we are truly passionate about in our lives. We need to be part dreamer, but mostly practical and methodical in the way we work to make our dreams come true. Next, I introduced four key elements that virtually all successful individuals have incorporated into their work careers: *momentum, consistency, patience* and *perseverance.*

Finally, I have shared my personal focus on staying *balanced* in all the important dimensions of our lives.

In Chapter Two, we will identify where we want to go and how we will get there.

"Designing Your Battle Plan"

Now that we have talked about the importance of dreaming and taking practical steps to turn your dreams into reality, let's focus on how you can get from A to Z. My first suggestion will not surprise you. Instead of focusing on going from A to Z, plan the "baby step" of going from A to B. Next, go from B to C, and then onward, one step at a time.

Unfortunately, many of us want to achieve our dreams in a single bound without really paying the dues that we know are usually required along the way. It's easy to see why. After all, we live in an age of instant gratification. We can obtain breakfast, lunch and dinner from the comfort of our cars at drive up windows at a variety of fast food convenience restaurants. We can drop off our clothes at the cleaners in the same fashion. There are drive-ups at some of the marriage chapels in Las Vegas – how convenient!

This "I want it now" mentality has led many individuals and families to dig themselves into credit card hell and ruin their credit histories. And as a society, we are all paying the consequences for our failure to eat the right portions of the right foods. Today, we have the highest incidence and percentages of adult and child obesity in our nation's history!

So many of us are forced to start with one or two strikes against us because we have made pretty major mistakes right out of the box. Before you can really make determined strides to accomplish your career objectives, you have to attend to these personal financial and health issues. If you find that you are on the wrong course, change it! The life you save just may be your own.

Assuming the above issues are not problematic for you, let's find a systematic way to chart your "roadmap" to where you want to go in your life. Once you have identified your objective, begin to list the "baby steps" that will get you to this destination. For instance, if you want to become a sales representative in the real estate industry, here are some items for your list:

Step 1   Enroll in real estate license course
Step 2   Attend required classes and take practice exams
Step 3   Schedule real estate sales license exam date
Step 4   Pass exam
Step 5   Find best broker for location and type of real estate sales that interests you (for example, if you are in a major city, determine the location and area that you want to specialize in, such as residential sales, investment and commercial sales, property management, property leasing, etc.)
Step 6   Interview with firms on your short list and select the best fit for your needs
Step 7   Go through your firm's training and orientation program
Step 8   Find an associate whom you can team up with or who can act as a mentor for you

Step 9   Volunteer for as much floor time as possible so
           you can find qualified buyers for the listings of
           your firm and other firms in the general location
           you have selected.
Step 10   Become an expert in all phases of your work by
           doing your homework (going out in the field and
           seeing properties, learning the techniques of
           appraisal by utilizing and comparing sale prices
           in the location of subject properties, learn the
           legal and business requirements that are
           involved in sales transactions, become familiar
           with the required obligations of buyers and
           sellers once the offer has been accepted and the
           property is in escrow before the close of the
           sale, etc.

Please note that the above listing of steps just scratches
the surface and is very general. However, as you can see,
it is progressive and each step builds on the step that
preceded it. This approach is one that is fundamentally
sound. It will take us where we want to go if we commit to
spending the time, effort and resources that are required
to make each step a reality.

Once I begin my coaching relationship with a new client, I
try to quickly determine my client's goals and facilitate
development of an action list of the steps necessary to
achieve the objectives. Often, my clients are already
established in their chosen professions and they have specific objectives that relate to their time and income levels.

For example, "George," one of my longest-term clients, told
me he wants to double his income this year so he can afford

to spend more quality time with his family and purchase the sports car of his dreams. My initial response might have disappointed him: I asked him to choose between making twice the amount of money and spending quality time with his family. That is because in his situation, I believed his two objectives to be mutually exclusive. To double his productivity in his current situation, he would need to dramatically increase his work hours (at least by twenty hours per week), and that would dramatically decrease the quality time he could spend with his family.

I suggested different goals: that he slightly increase the time he works but also eliminate low-productivity activities that might be keeping his income down. Then he could increase the quality time he spends with his family. He still wants to purchase the sports car, though, and if he does work smarter this year, he might be able to pull it off!

I happen to be a person who makes lists. It is easier for me to keep my focus if I write daily lists of objectives. When we are establishing our objectives, we need to ask ourselves, "Why do I want to accomplish this particular goal?" and "How will I benefit on a short-term and long-term basis?"

For instance, if our goal is to lose weight over a given period of time, what are the benefits of a successful outcome? First, we will be in better health and that is good in both the short and the long term. Second, our weight loss will let us wear smaller clothes, and everyone in our society knows that better appearance and style are important. Studies prove that a pleasing appearance results in better treatment. Need I say more? Finally, our weight loss will probably enhance our self-esteem.

This will give us tangible satisfaction – first, from accomplishing our goal, and then from seeing the results in our improved image (in our mirrors and in the eyes of those who now are treating us with more respect).

I want you to know, though, that I do not think less of my fellow human beings because of a weight problem or other physical characteristics. I believe in facilitating success, and if I can motivate someone to achieve their dreams and objectives, I'm there!

Let's look at another type of plan – a specific reward plan for one of my clients. "Susan" wanted to be more productive so she and her husband could remodel their kitchen in a time frame of two years. We discussed how she could use her time more productively, and we decided to give her a tangible daily reminder of her "mission" – a photo of her ideal kitchen, from a design or architecture magazine, to post where she would see it each day.

A week later, the photo was in place near Susan's workstation to remind her what she was working to achieve. She started to work longer and more productive hours, and her numbers rose more than 20% over a sustained period of time, even though the economy and the printing industry had been mired in a prolonged recession!

And not long ago, Susan told me her latest news. Not only had she earned enough to finance the new kitchen remodeling, she and her husband were able to buy a new home with an upgraded kitchen already included in the mix!

When a client of mine achieves a sought-after goal, I feel like a coach who has just taken her team to a championship title. That's how I'll be feeling when you reap the same kind of return on your efforts that Susan did.

Now let's go back to review and to discuss the components of our action plan. As you will note, the examples that I use happen to refer to salespeople, but you can apply them easily to your own current or future career. That is because selling, teamwork and relating to people are components in virtually all careers.

- Set your goal. It needs to be realistic and attainable. Remember, it's A to B, not to Z!
- Establish your time frame. How long will your effort take? What do you need to have in place so you can start today?
- Determine your first action steps. For example, if you want to make more money, start with your proven accounts. Can you expand the amount of business you do with them this year? Have you bothered to ask them how much business they will do this year? Have you stayed in contact with your key account person and/or team?
- Monitor and track your progress on a daily, weekly, monthly, quarterly and yearly basis. Become a master of follow-through. Try to stay objective about your own strengths and weaknesses, and those of your company.
- Evaluate where you and your firm are in the scheme of things. If you are constantly ahead of the curve and pushing a reluctant management team, maybe you need to join a more progressive team. After all, you know what happens to sales people who consistently miss their quotas! Remember, success is a two-way street. You must consider all factors in your quest to be the best at your position and in your industry.

- Stay balanced in the other dimensions of your life, because your job is not your life. It is just one element. If you become dramatically more productive, making significant gains relatively quickly, this will allow you many new options in your daily life. For instance, you will be able to indulge yourself and your loved ones with thoughtful expressions of devotion. It's a cliché, but roses are there to savor every day!

Now, perhaps you have heard of the 80/20 law. It says that 20% of sales associates and firms account for 80% of business. Why do the other 80% of sales associates and firms let this happen? Because they rationalize! The following list will explain. It contains just a few of the excuses I have heard in my corporate coaching practice in the last seven years, and they apply to the personal and professional aspirations of many people around us.

The Top Ten List of Excuses:

1. "I don't have enough time to get everything done."
2. "I'm just big boned. There's nothing I can do about it."
3. "My client's business is not doing well this year."
4. "My sales manager doesn't understand me."
5. "I don't get the support I need from my spouse."
6. "There's just too much traffic out there to fight to get to the gym on a regular basis."
7. "I can't seem to get a fair break."
   (This is a variation of, "It's who you know.")
8. "I just can't find a good man/woman to meet."
9. "If only I hadn't grown up in such a dysfunctional family."
10. "There's just too much stress and pressure in my job. My inner child wants to spend more time at recess."

All right, I admit to having a little fun with that last excuse; I haven't actually heard anyone say it yet. But I think you get the idea. It really is so easy to blame others when we don't reach our objectives. Actually, society gives us a lot of encouragement for this type of behavior. Most TV talk shows feature grownups acting like children. Today, everyone fears being accused of saying anything that could offend a listener. I'm sorry, but in my practice, my first principle is, "Take responsibility for your outcome. Tell me what you want to accomplish and we will agree on the path, but you are in charge of your destiny!"

I practice what I preach, and I hold myself accountable to a high objective standard. I have little use for phony excuses. It is true that we all encounter adversity; but we must strive to overcome it. Here is an example of success in the face of adversity. It is the story of Olympic hero Cliff Meidl, and he related it at one of my printing sales workshops.

When Cliff was just 20 years old, 30,000 volts of electricity coursed through him in a construction accident, and immediately after that he suffered three cardiac arrest episodes. When he awoke from all of this, he was told he would probably lose both legs above the knees.

Fortunately, Cliff's parents found an amazing plastic surgeon who miraculously saved his legs in 15 surgeries over 15 months. Here is a person who could honestly say he was dealt a pretty tough hand. So what did he do? He proved everyone wrong. Not only did he learn to walk again, he actually went on to make the U.S. Olympic kayak team – and not just once, but twice! In kayaking, upper body strength is paramount. Cliff was the proud American flagbearer who led the U.S. Team into the Opening Ceremonies at the 2000 Sydney Olympic Games as 2 billion people watched on TV around the world!

This exceptional human being's outstanding example makes a point. Yes, all of us experience setbacks daily. Yes, life is not fair. But if you have that spark in your heart and soul, and you are driven to succeed, then nothing can stop you from attaining your goals. If you are willing to commit to your plan and to spend the necessary time and energy, success will be yours!

So what have we learned?

First, that usually it is best to focus on getting from A to B instead of trying to get from A to Z. Also, that we need to temper our objectives with a little bit of common sense and discipline. We don't want to spend our way or eat our way into lifestyles that are self-defeating. In addition, we all know the importance of appearance and personal image in this society of ours.

We also learned that when we choose to make changes that will enhance our self-esteem, and when we persist, then we can succeed! And we found that we can boost our chances of succeeding when we "buy in" and when we are willing to make our programs a top priority to us and to our family.

We learned about my friends "George" and "Susan" and their personal aspirations for more productive lives. We talked about how to approach our battle plan and listed examples of a specific beginning plan and the components and considerations of a battle plan. In addition, we listed common excuses that we all hear every day.

Finally, I shared the story of the uncommon courage and dedication of Cliff Meidl and his journey back from devastating injuries. His inspirational example demonstrates the amazing power of the human spirit. Cliff was faced with a life-changing catastrophe that challenged his very life. We need to give thanks each day for our many blessings and to seek the strength to attempt to be the "best that we can be" in our own lives.

In Chapter Three we will discuss fundamental concepts that we all need to practice. I have found that this section is valuable no matter where you are in your career plan. For the novice, this is essential to get our candidate into the "game." For the seasoned pro, you may just find that you have forgotten a thing or two that will help you make the right impression for your most important client. Read on!

"Focus On
Your Behavior"

Now we're ready to hit the ground running and to begin to make things happen in our lives! However, before we get too excited and carried away with zeal, we must remember the most important concept of all when it comes to one's business career. This concept comes from my writing partner Tom who received this bit of advice when he was starting his firm:

"Your business career is not a sprint – it is a marathon."

So, before you get too involved in the pursuit of overnight success and riches, please remember the importance of being fundamentally sound in everything that you do from the beginning of your career until your retirement days. Tom likes to tell the story of the new basketball recruits who were addressed in their opening workouts at UCLA by the "Wizard of Westwood," Coach John Wooden. He won 10 NCAA basketball titles in just 12 years and then retired at age 65 at the absolute pinnacle of his profession.

What was one of the first topics addressed by this genius of the hardwood? To the recruits' amazement, he demonstrated the proper way for a UCLA basketball player to tie his shoes and wear his socks! Although these recruits were among the best prep players in the land, Coach Wooden wanted them to be sound in every aspect of their games (beginning with their shoes.) So, get ready to learn from the ground up in the sales arena!

This listing of our 100 focus points will address your behavior, your sales skills and your longevity in going about your work. These focus points are the result of the authors' collective experience and observation in the business world. We encourage you to take these suggested focus points to heart. You won't be sorry.

"Focus on Your Behavior"

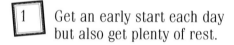

1 Get an early start each day
but also get plenty of rest.

If you are on the West Coast and your work is not merely local but also includes some clients who are based on the East Coast, 6 a.m. is really 9 a.m. for your East Coast clients. Don't give them another reason to go elsewhere. How impressive is it when an East Coast client calls you at 6:15 a.m. and finds you up and working? It has to make them think, "I've got the right person handling my business!" Also, there's something about getting an early start to your day that just makes you more productive – when you get the most out of the day on a consistent basis.

2 Get enough rest and be fresh and alert for your meetings.

Obviously, you can't continue to burn the candle on both ends and hope to be very effective. When you "buy in" to getting up early, you also buy in to getting to bed at an earlier time as well so you can get the sleep you need. If you are in your early twenties, you're probably smiling right now and thinking back to the all-nighters that you recently pulled in school. But when you are no longer twenty-something, you will actually need that sleep to function.

 3 Show up. (It's amazing what can happen!)

We all have had to start something new in our lives at one point or another. Often, that can make us quite apprehensive. We worry, about what can go wrong, and everything might seem foreign and impossible to master. When we face these situations in our lives, the first step is just to show up. It is truly amazing how a friendly smile and demeanor can open up doors for us if we just show up and make the effort.

4 ALWAYS be on time!

Despite the rush hour traffic that everyone encounters in a large city, this is one factor we can usually control. Being on time says something about you. It says you care enough about your job and your employer to be there, whether for an important client meeting or just the start of your workday.

Be a good listener. This is one of the traits usually lacking in those who fail!

In my sales workshops, I create hypothetical situations that involve salespersons and clients. A salesperson who fails to respond to a client's expressed needs WILL LOSE THAT ACCOUNT. One of the most important characteristics of a successful human being and salesperson is the ability to focus on the needs of others. This empathy is invaluable. Often it is one of the chief building blocks of a successful long-term sales relationship. If you learn nothing else from this book, please take this concept to heart.

 Be yourself and let your natural personality emerge in your work.

Very few of us function at a maximum level when we constantly feel constricted. For a new salesperson, it is as important to learn how to relax and be yourself as it is to "learn the new ropes" of your craft. When that magic moment arrives and you begin to actually enjoy your work (some of us never get to this point unfortunately), a whole new wave of confidence will come over you. Suddenly, you will "get it" and understand that you really CAN SUCCEED IN YOUR CAREER! This is another fundamental element that is vital to your success. It will immediately enhance your sense of self-esteem and the personal fulfillment your work provides.

7 | Make your handshake a firm one –
but don't break bones.

A firm handshake conveys a sense of professionalism and will helps to make the desired impression when you meet someone new. It's also something that just comes naturally to many of us. Do you have a firm handshake? There's just something solid about someone who looks you in the eye and firmly shakes your hand. But be careful to don't overdo it and cause the recipient any pain. Many of us make that serious mistake.

8 | Smile and look directly into the eyes of your
clients and associates.

Our eyes are the portals of our bodies. When you flash a friendly smile and look into another person's eyes in a friendly way, you are accepting them and validating their importance to you. Conversely, if you avoid another person's eyes, you are acting as if you have something to hide or as if they don't merit your full consideration or attention.

9 | Say "thank you" when someone goes out of
his or her way for you.

Yes, we do know how obvious this tip is. But you wouldn't believe how many individuals continually fail to acknowledge their family members, friends, associates and even clients for the courtesies and special consider-ations they give on a daily basis. Such failures and omis-sions are simply "kindness-killers." Virtually no one will continue to extend such favors and gracious treatment to such clueless recipients.

10 Make a real effort to get along with the other people in your office.

Just when you thought we were through with the obvi-ous... Sadly, many promising careers get shot down because of petty behavior in the office. The best way to get a perspective on this problem is to compare it with something similar in a different environment. We all know enough to avoid getting into an argument or brawl in a public place. So why do we allow another individual, who might be on his or her way out anyway to prod us into constant bickering or snide remarks in the office? The bottom line for this type of problem is to avoid it in the first place. It doesn't really matter who started it. However, if we're talking about a definite injustice or a violation of your rights as an employee, then you must go to your manager and stand up for yourself.

11 Be there for others when they need some assistance, support or counsel.

Working in an office environment can be similar in some ways to what we experienced in school. Sometimes, a co-worker will need assistance or you yourself might. It is a good idea to adopt a team approach to your company and "be there" for others when they need support. Sometimes, it is enough just to talk to someone about a pressing problem or other matter. Obviously, your goal is not to become the resident pseudo-therapist but if you can help someone, do.

12 Be a good sport and treat others fairly in competitive bidding situations, etc.

As a wise man once said, "You only have one chance to make a good first impression." As you will quickly discover, your given industry really is a small world – so act accordingly. Be fair with others, even competitors for a sale, and treat them the way you would want to be treated. After all, by next year, you might want to work with the competition, or the competition might be working with your firm. If you need more convincing on this point, I can remind you that it is not only the right thing to do, it is good business!

13 Establish a routine that allows you to be productive.

We are all creatures of habit. Some of us are more habit-oriented than others. As a result, I believe in doing everything in our control to ensure the outcome we desire. When we are beginning a new transition in our lives, such as getting our first job or moving to a new one, we want to do everything possible to reach and exceed the performance levels that we or others (such as our sales manager) have established. We've already discussed getting an early start on the day and making sure that we are well rested and always on time. Other winning strategies can include avoiding negative habits such as web surfing, which not only wastes our time but cheats our employers out of time we should be spending on the job.

Do a personal inventory of all your job-related tasks as well as any negative habits, such as long lunches, drinks during the day, excessive personal business on the job, etc. Once you have completed this list, check for your positive habits. For instance, you probably have set regular times for staying current in your industry by reading your business trades; "cold calls"; a physical conditioning program. You might also have set regularly scheduled lunches with your clients; regular catch-up calls with your "warm list" of potential clients and regular activities in your community involving those who can use your services.

As you've noticed here, I'm stressing the word "regular" – because that's the way it needs to be. You need to develop a systematic approach to the work you do so it soon will become second nature. As you might expect, when you reach that point, you should begin to experience much more success. That's because your efforts have a foundation to them and you're building upon the work you've already done. When my clients get to this point of critical mass, they just start selling more and more. All I can say is that this approach usually works for my clients. If you get to this point and do not experience more sales productivity, you will want to find out what other factors are holding you back.

14 Keep a positive mental attitude and remember that your future is based on your performance!

You will find a recurring theme throughout this book: we emphasize the value of staying in a positive mental attitude as much as possible. It would be wonderful if all of us could incorporate this attitude all the time. It does cost us money if we fail to exhibit this approach regularly in our work.

Sports analogies and examples are quite effective in the business world. That's because the fit is such a precise one. Tom likes to compare players to all employees and teams to companies like the one you work for or own. Tom also compares sports games to the sales results and new accounts that you and your firms acquire. In every game, there is a winner and a loser, and thus an immediate outcome.

There's even a sports analogy for my profession and your managers. They can be compared to teams' head coaches and assistant coaches. You can see where I'm going with this one. Sports team owners and the owners of the other companies are in a virtually identical position. When a professional sports team wins on a consistent basis, all is good with the world! Players and coaches get bonuses, contract extensions and lots of recognition within the team organization and league. However, if the franchise starts losing, heads will roll! Players get released and the team's coaches get their walking papers.

In other words, the worlds of both business and sports focus on results. You can expect rewards when you win and unpleasant consequences when you lose.

Speaking of expectations, this leads into another of Tom's sports metaphors in the business world. A great sports team will develop a positive collective psychology and dynamic. Many of the members of the team expect to win and every additional victory reinforces the team's collective expectation so that individual players begin to find ways to deliver this outcome when the game is "on the line."

Being positive is a difficult proposition. Often, we might desire to vent at someone who has just pushed our buttons or done something clearly offensive. However, if we have fully incorporated a positive approach to every aspect of our lives, we won't allow another's thoughtless act to interfere with or control our reactions. This involves our shedding of the normal reactive point of view that we see every day while driving or in some other public arena where rudeness is on display.

 Maintain a consistent approach to your work.

As we've said, consistency is an extremely important element in our lives. By being consistent you will be able to stay focused and on track. Others will begin to view you in a positive light when they see that you actually do follow through on your commitments and your promises to them. What could be more important than this? Briefly, here are some easy ways to stay consistent:
a. Make lists.
b. Establish regular routines (for your workouts and your cold calling, for example).
c. Build in rewards when you have completed difficult tasks.

d. Practice time management priority systems and allocate your high grades ("A" and "B") to necessary tasks that need to get done in a timely fashion.

 Evaluate your progress on a daily, weekly, monthly, quarterly and yearly basis.

One of the nice things I enjoy about coaching motivated and dedicated individuals is witnessing their systematic refining of their objectives and their plans to achieve these objectives. Keeping daily time logs helps them allocate the amount of time they spend on each project and client.

As days and weeks pass, my clients begin to form an accurate picture of how they are spending their time. Once they see which clients and projects have been the most productive and least productive, they can make changes and adjustments. But only complete and total honesty in keeping these logbooks will result in true and honest insights.

 Don't overlook those closest to you.

Throwing yearly appreciation lunch events, usually around the holiday season, is a great way for me to show my close friends and clients how much they mean to me. I can interact with them and spend quality time with them at this wonderful and special time of the year. Recently, one of my closest friends came up to me after the luncheon and informed me that now that she knew more about my sales coaching services, she believed her major Fortune 500 firm could benefit from them. She was right, and I did get a new and exciting client as a result!

So, don't forget to tell those who are closest to you what you do for a living. However, there is always a catch to these "close encounters of the family and friend "kind." Be extra careful when you work with family, friends and relatives, because you never want to jeopardize these personal and cherished relationships. If you know a particular family member or friend to be a little sensitive or difficult, be extra careful and think about asking a trusted employee or associate in your office to handle this family member or friend's business.

18 Reach out for your client's charitable projects, if possible.

When your client's children are selling their raffle tickets or Girl Scout cookies, make sure you place your orders in a timely and substantial way. Just consider these little gestures as an investment and a way of saying "thanks" to a valued client. Obviously, you will need to use your good judgment and common sense when it comes to such items. As a rule, don't mention your charity projects to your clients.

19 Avoid the minefields!

We've all heard horror stories about inappropriate behavior that got our former associates fired or nearly fired.

None of the following trouble areas should come as much of a surprise but you'd be surprised what people do.

a. If you drink, use discretion with your intake of alcohol. Holiday parties have harmed many people's careers because they drink to excess. Also, if your spouse or significant other is a risk in this regard, you should probably attend alone.

b. Office romance. Need I say anything more? If you're dating the boss, you're playing with fire!

c. Don't play favorites with the staff or your associates. And don't favor one client over another unless that one client is *the* client.

d. Please be careful with legal and business compliance issues. Always dot your i's and cross your t's when it comes to things that can get you (and/or your firm) fined, sued or dumped by a client.

e. Always keep tabs on your primary client's activities and new friends. If your chief client who accounts for half of your firm's business is a fishing enthusiast, you should be with him on his yearly fishing expedition and providing some perks along the way in accordance with law or trade custom, of course.

f. Careful with that cell phone of yours! (Please note later focus point on this.)

g. Careful when interacting with your client in social and public circles. (Always show respect and always act in a socially graceful manner by never failing to introduce your clients and their spouse, companion, etc.)

h. Never gossip about anyone in the office. And don't talk about your firm's confidential business, or your client's business, in public settings in a less than discreet manner (for instance, in an elevator, restroom or compromised dining setting.)

20 | Don't ever discriminate.

Not only is discrimination usually illegal and just stupid, it also can cost you dearly down the road when someone whom you once discarded becomes your new boss or the new decision-maker for your largest client! One of the great things about our free enterprise system is that it rewards initiative and hard work. I know that all of my owner and sales manager clients would give their eye-teeth for a great salesperson – man or woman and of any ethnic and religious heritage under the stars. A successful sales professional is worth his or her weight in gold. This will never change.

Tom points out that often, individuals from other countries and cultures appreciate the freedom and opportunity that we all have on a daily basis all the more because it's something they never had. As a result, the "buy in" from such individuals can be overwhelming.

21 | Never lie or misrepresent critical information.

We've all heard of executives or other leaders who told a "little white lie" on their resumes or omitted a critical fact in a business transaction or setting. No one is above the reach and power of the truth. As a result, verify what you represent as fact to buyers and sellers and other key parties of high-ticket transactions. The reputation that you save just might be your own. Also, don't exaggerate or over-promise a client, because you will be the one who disappoints that client if you fail to deliver what you promised. In addition, this flaw can lead to your company failing to make a substantial profit if you give away the store to get the business. Be a team player and not a doormat in your client relationships!

 Make the time to assist others in need by volunteering for worthy community and industry causes.

Whenever I discuss something of this nature, it is a given that I believe the first reason for your involvement is because you really want to do something for others in your community. However, why not choose a charity cause or organization that is backed by your industry or the movers and shakers in your community? This will enable you to work with them in a more natural manner and allow you to get to know them on a personal level as well. I just believe in maximizing your efforts if possible, because there are only 168 hours in each week.

 There is such a thing as "karma" so make yours good karma!

I do believe in the principle of good and bad karma. Why not have the good stuff going for you? When you build a foundation on solid ground and you treat others in the way that you would wish to be treated, the word of mouth will build and you will receive benefits from these good works.

Conversely, when you spend your life "doing unto others before they can do unto you," bad things will happen. I can guarantee it. When someone is wronged, there is that basic human need for revenge. I'm here to tell you that revenge can take many forms. Some of us out there in the world don't seem to "get it" – and then, when the day of reckoning and/or payback arrives, they don't have a clue as to why these terrible things are happening to them!

24 | Be conservative in your projections when starting out in your career or new venture.

We've all heard stories about an inventor who came up with some incredible idea and started a little side venture that sprouted into the next giant international corporation. Well, it can happen if you actually put your ideas to work. One thing that will help you along the way is to be conservative in your allocation of resources in the start up phases.

Why not start your enterprise in your home and/or garage? If you absolutely need a business address, rent a post office box or mail service at one of the office suite firms if you can. (The suite companies may not be in your location, but anyone can rent a post office box.) If you're starting a new venture that involves more than yourself and your immediate family, you will need an office; but just dial it down a couple of notches until you really know that the business to sustain you will be there. Keep yourself on a tight budget while you take your business to the next level.

Naturally, there are a couple of exceptions to this basic

premise. If you are real estate sales professional, your satellite office is your automobile. I would advise you to save and scrimp and somehow manage to lease or acquire the most elegant car that you can afford. In this case, you will be asking your clients to trust your judgment and advice in (for most of them) the biggest investment they will ever make. It will be in your favor if you look like you've done this before. Also, all sales and business professionals need to dress in a professional manner as well. There will be more specifics to come on this, but suffice to say that you need to project a completely professional presence with your clients and associates.

25 │ Make the most of your time in the office.

The next couple of points deal with the time we spend in and out of the office. While we want to be cordial and respectful to others in our office environments, we also need to focus on what truly benefits us – making sales! So be careful not to get caught up in office politics or too many administrative tasks. Keep your eye on the ball and make every minute count. For the beginning real estate sales person, covering the floor calls makes sense. It is an obligation that is usually equally shared (at least by the newer associates who need to find potential qualified buyers). However, be sure and get out of the office so you can spend "face time" with your best clients and when you are in the office, focus on your sales calls and other sales-related activities that can help you exceed your sales goals.

26 Avoid the common bad habits that will drop your production level.

Here are some of the most common "time wasters":

a. Surfing the Internet. Some current studies have estimated that employees spend up to ten hours a week surfing while at work. That's 500 hours per year that they're not working!

b. Making excessive personal phone calls while on the job.

c Spending too much time at the water cooler or in the restroom.

d. Spending too much time socializing with administrative staff or colleagues and not working.

e. Taking care of personal chores while on the job.

Stop making excuses to your manager and/or spouses as to why the production level is not there. Take charge of your workday starting now! After all, there is only a limited amount of time during the day when you can sell to your potential clients. Use your "prime time" to sell and ask yourself what other tasks can be done after hours.

27 Maintain good client contact, especially with your best clients.

We all have primary clients who account for much of our incomes. These "keeper" clients need to know we are there for them. They need to be our first priority in our workdays. Many of my best clients are too busy for lunch. So they really respond when I bring lunch to them! I get face time and they get convenience (and a nutritious meal).

Make an effort to keep yourself in front of your key clients in quality ways such as these:

a. Provide critical updates concerning areas of interest to them.

b. Avoid e-mailing jokes to your clients unless your client is somewhat unique and has a penchant for the latest joke. Being a comedian is not the perception you want. Busy executives already overwhelmed by communications often find it an annoyance.

c Provide your clients with requested bid and quote info and the latest requested materials (including presentations and demos).

d. Put together your own in-house newsletter list so you can share your latest accomplishments with your "warm" recipients.

e. If the material that you are providing to your client is timely and important, always opt for the greatest impact possible – either deliver it in person, or if the client is out of town, overnight it for next morning delivery. This does make a difference!

| 28 | Avoid the negative people in the workplace and in your personal life. |

We all know who they are. When we or one of our colleagues has just completed a record-breaking sales month, they are the ones who snicker, whine or make excuses about why they would have achieved results "if only life was fair." On any team, there are usually over-achievers, average achievers and under-achievers. Great teams are marked by great numbers of over-achievers who will not settle for anything less than winning championships. What do you want to be?

If you decide you want to achieve great things, then you must buy in and commit to the program that you and/or your coach designs. Also, you will need to prepare yourself for the reaction of some people close to you who will not be able to handle your new success. We find these people in our offices and even in our homes. I call these individuals "de-motivators" and saboteurs. However, some of my clients still consider them to be their friends.

Unfortunately, many of our friends like us most when we are not too successful in our work. Many of these individuals are actually threatened by this success because it confronts them with their own demons and failures. Change is difficult. When one of my clients makes the commitment to be the best person possible and sets personal and professional goals, I am there to help my client make it come true!

Be prepared for the true cost and sacrifice that will be involved.

 29 Be gracious in your dealings with your clients and colleagues. This is a lost but profitable art!

When is the last time someone really went out of his way for you to provide something you needed, and did so in the best way? Bet you really appreciated that effort, didn't you? You can see where I am going with this. Many of us need to become much more aware of the efforts and needs of those around us.

Sometimes, all that is required is to communicate our concerns. At other times, we need to demonstrate our caring. When someone we care about loses a family member or close friend, be there for them. Acts of kindness at critical times will always be appreciated and rewarded. Get creative and find ways to do things for clients and others that really touch them. After all, one of the most important fundamentals in today's competitive sales environment is that sales are a result of your relationship with your clients. Never forget this ultimate truth.

30 Get your phone calls returned by offering good news.

Remember an important but simple fact of human nature – all of us like to receive good news. When you're dealing with the decision-maker's "gatekeeper" (or a voice mail), just let them know you've got good news to share. But you will need to have something that will actually interest your intended decision-maker!

31 Be mindful of today's rules for office conduct.

Today's successful sales professionals will avoid jeopardizing their careers by entering into a romantic involvement with a boss or colleague. They will avoid questionable displays of affection for a staff member or other party. They will be extra careful about the language they use in business communications.

No matter what you really meant and even if you thought it was funny and/or harmless, it can get you fired. Each day brings new examples of tasteless attempts at humor that were included in official firm e-mails or advisories, and the outcome is usually devastating for the offending party.

 Avoid career deal-breakers such as:

a. Driving under the influence. Obviously, this behavior may take other human lives and put you away for an extended vacation. However, many of us don't realize that many states now employ .08 alcohol blood level standards that can be reached in as little as two or even one drink (if your bartender is looking for a tip and is generous with the portions). Unfortunately, often the person with a problem is the last to know and if you are one of these unfortunate individuals, it may take going through a DUI to cure you (or not).

b. Financial improprieties (even cheating on your expense account can bite you). Be scrupulous and get approvals from your management before taking any advantage in any way.

c Bad-mouthing your firm or your manager, your associate or a rival. One fact of life that everyone in the entertainment industry is aware of: You never know who will be in charge in the future. So be very careful not to let your emotions run away with you when bad things happen. Some firms have ruined their own reputations by bad-mouthing successful employees or representatives who had the audacity to leave the firm. This type of behavior won't impress anyone who matters, and it could get you or the firm sued!

33 Roll up your sleeves, because over-achievers don't work 9-to-5!

If you want to be the best, get ready to work harder than you have ever worked in your life. If you are a recent high school or college (or professional school) graduate, the party is over and now is the time to really get serious about your future!

Highly successful individuals work long hours. There is no getting around this necessity. If you have just joined a top law firm and you want to make partner-shareholder status in seven years, get ready to work 60-70 hours per week so you can bill a minimum of 200 hours per month.

Remember the time log process I mentioned? One reason I insisted upon it is it will help you see where you really are in terms of time and productivity. Sadly, many of us who think we are working 35-45 hours per week are truly only working 20-25 hours because of the negative habits and distractions that creep into our days.

Obviously, your work ethic will have a strong impact on those who are closest to you. There will need to be a support team around you in the form of a spouse who will pick up the slack for you at home if you are married and with children.

34 Show respect for your clients and practice proper social etiquette!

In today's current climate of reality television and incredibly tasteless behavior in the most public and unexpected places, we can be tempted to let our guard down in our business lives. Be careful! Your clients are still the people who are responsible for your salaries and commissions. If you do something to cause offense, you're on shaky ground. And sometimes, it's what you don't do that can offend.

If you have not done this before, consider buying a recommended social etiquette book and read it cover to cover. I guarantee you that you will immediately spot some things that you are doing incorrectly in given situations. Pay special attention to the section on introductions and make sure that you are courteous and gracious in your dealings with all other individuals (especially your clients and bosses) at all times.

Obviously, you know your clients. If you have established a certain give and take that is working, don't change it. However, if some of your behavior is borderline, start adjusting that attitude. For example, do you stand up when your client joins you for lunch or dinner? This is a no-brainer. Just do it!

35 Now about those cell phones!

We all agree that we want to project the most professional image possible in our work lives. Part of being a business professional is how we conduct ourselves in the presence of others. Why do perfectly rational business executives engage in absolutely rude behavior when using the cell phone? We all have our stories. The guy at our bank who made his teller wait while he finished his call right in front of her. Not only was his behavior extremely disrespectful to that teller, but he made each and every one of us in line wait a little bit longer as well.

And most of us have experienced near-collisions on our busy city streets and freeways because our fellow drivers were preoccupied with their phone conversations or attempts at dialing their cell phones!

Be careful about abusing cell phone etiquette because this problem is reaching the boiling point in our society. Just use your common sense. And please learn how to put your cell on vibrate when you are in your next meeting or other situation where the ringing is an annoyance.

36 | No one is immune to the consequences of poor driving habits.

Think twice before cutting off too many other drivers on the way to your client's office, because one of those drivers just may be your client! Also, driving is not a right, it is a privilege. Too many tickets and accidents can not only cost you money, they can jeopardize your license. Often, one of the primary reasons for our speeding is our tardiness. Start giving yourself an extra 15 minutes to get where you need to go, and an extra 30 minutes if you are going to see your client or attend an important meeting. This one change will do wonders for you.

37   Manage that temper of yours.

Believe me, I realize that we live in extremely stressful times. After September 11, 2001, our lives changed forever. Many of us are under extreme amounts of pressure. Our decisions and performance can affect many other people besides ourselves and our families. But there is never an excuse to "lose it" in any circumstance!

If you discover that you have anger management problems, get help. Most firms are much more progressive in the way they deal with this. The first step for you is a personal assessment and inventory. Have you had outbursts of anger in the past with a family member, friend, associate or the guy who just cut you off on the freeway?

One little coping trick for avoiding harmful blowups is to just stop yourself before you erupt by calling a "time out" and leaving the room for a few minutes. Naturally, you won't put your hands in a "T" and signal! Rather, you will just excuse yourself and go outside to make a cell call or go to the restroom. It doesn't matter what you do, just defuse the situation by leaving for a few minutes until calmer heads prevail.

However, I am not a therapist. So please do seek help through the proper channels. There have never been more tools to deal with these problems that can interfere with (or end) our productive careers.

One final word…

If your boss is a screamer, try a different tack. Tom once had a boss who would erupt when his subordinates reported to him. After experiencing one such eruption himself, Tom decided to try an alternative approach before looking for another position. From that point on, Tom's reports were always in written form to his boss. Guess what? It worked. Tom never again experienced a problem with that boss. In fact, he had a long and successful association with the firm, and the boss complimented him in front of many key clients and associates. At the time, that job experience was pivotal in Tom's career.

However, again, use your judgment. If you are saddled with a boss or supervisor who is a spoiled child and throws tantrums, think about using your network of friends and associates to network right out of that awful situation.

38 | Dress like a professional.

This focus point applies to the corporate culture. It dictates professional attire. For a man, that means a suit (or sport coat and matching dress slacks), a necktie and shined shoes. For a woman, it means a tasteful dress or appropriate pantsuit, with matching accessories. For everyone, hair must be groomed and styled, and general appearance must indicate taste and success.

Plan for warm days by having a personal kit to use, when needed, after lunch. But avoid the common mistake, which both men and women make, of carrying too much "stuff." When men carry too many items in their pockets (pants or jacket), and when women stuff their purses, they give the impression of being disorganized. That's especially true when they waste their time and the client's by rummaging through their clutter.

Naturally, the corporate culture and the industry norms you observe can temper these rules. For example, if you work at a company that practices "casual Friday" dress days, you can participate. Also, you might work in the entertainment industry, which marches to a different drum. Our advice is to be aware of your environment and adapt to it.

Also, I don't advise women to dress too provocatively. Be sure to avoid plunging necklines and to keep skirts or hemlines stylish but not too short.

Make sure your clothes are not too tight and are not torn or faded. You would be amazed by what we have observed over the years in terms of stocking tears, ripped trousers, unzipped flies. You get the idea.

If you wear a hairpiece, do invest in a high-quality one. Nothing is more distracting than a bad hairpiece. Even TV commercials ridicule men who wear obvious hairpieces. A bad hairpiece is a reason for people not to take you seriously – and that's not the impression you want to create!

39 Be the professional in your office environment.

Even if the protocol for your sales presentations is to take clients into a closing office or a conference room, they could still end up in your office or cubicle. So make sure your work space is always fastidiously neat and organized. The same rule applies to real estate and automobile professionals. Get rid of old newspapers, wadded Kleenex, coffee cups, etc.

As we've said earlier, make your automobile one of your best investments. Don't mortgage your future by buying or leasing a car that is totally beyond your means, but do think about the image you want to project to your clients. This is especially true in real estate; many sales associates and brokers drive luxury automobiles because the car is where they and their clients will spend most of their time together.

Also, when you open up your briefcase or leather bag, make sure everything is neat and in its proper place. Don't be searching for papers or fumbling around when you need to be closing your client. When it comes to this step in the sales process, don't leave anything to chance. Care enough to go the extra mile. Prepare your surroundings and presentation materials (your offer forms and disclosure information) for presentation to your client in the most professional manner possible. If you expect your clients to sign or complete an offer form, you'd better have a pen – and a backup! – ready to hand to them.

Just remember, all these rules are for our own success in sales. After all, it's hard enough to close a deal in the first place without shooting ourselves in the foot!

 ## Watch that body language!

As we've all read, some surveys actually conclude that body language is the most important and determinative form of communication. Don't spend entire days in front of the mirror, but do be aware of that! Make sure that when you enter a room, you project a positive and confident air with each step and action. Don't slouch your shoulders or fidget around in a distracting way. To find a role model, watch a movie with a classic movie star such as Cary Grant, Gregory Peck, Grace Kelly or Loretta Young. We can all learn from them.

So what have we learned in Chapter Three?

We've learned some practical but crucial fundamental rules concerning our behavior and the behavior of those around us. No matter where you are in your career, these focus points can help you avoid pitfalls and can provide you with the meaningful edge you need to stay one step ahead of the competition! Now it's on to Chapter Four where we will address focus points that relate to sales.

"Sales Focus Points"

Now we're ready to move into the world of sales. Bring on the focus points!

 Do your daily and weekly homework and stay current on all aspects of your product or services.

It's important to try to stay one or more steps ahead of your clients' current business considerations. By focusing on your clients' interests, you can begin to develop a knack for anticipating their needs on a regular basis. Also, when you're meeting a new client for the first time, try to gather as much intelligence as you can for that first pivotal meeting.

Here's an example. One of my clients set up a meeting with "Fred," a new client of his who had been the right-hand man of a now-deceased power broker. My client prepared for the meeting by reading a book by Fred's deceased mentor, so he could use a phrase or two that would ring true with Fred, the new man in control. My client's strategy paid off and he got the new business!

42 | Don't dwell on the past. Live in the now and the future.

This is a very important concept. Please make sure you think about it. Most people who've been in business for a few years must deal with projects and clients who have disappointed them. We need to get past these experiences so we don't carry baggage into new relationships. And we usually learn more from failures than victories. So don't dwell on a loss, learn to move on!

Also, if we've had some outstanding years at a company, we might start to rest on our laurels a bit. We can fool ourselves into believing that we're special because of our past achievements, even if now we're below our expected sales levels. As all of us know, we need to be outstanding every year. The saying, "What have you done for us lately?" does apply to our sales careers. Get used to this and deal with it! This is just the way it is.

One of Tom's coping tools is to set his own expectations and goals higher than the stated objectives of his clients. That way, he'll always be reaching above and beyond what they might expect.

43 | Go the extra mile in serving your clients' needs.

One of the best ways to do this is to follow through on all action items that you and your client have established. Address any client concerns when they arise. Be as attentive as possible to your clients' requests. Always write them down immediately. Then keep a constant flow of communication going, so you can let the client know as soon as you satisfy each request.

There usually is a rhythm or dynamic at work with each client. Having had long relationships with these individuals, we've shared many experiences and probably bonded in a number of ways. But it is valuable to keep renewing the relationship – so find new, creative ways to increase clients' business or to save time for them. We can't allow ourselves the luxury of taking their business for granted. We must always remember that our clients are accountable for the profits they earn. Their loyalty to us will always be conditioned upon the quality of our efforts for them.

Here are a few tips on ways to keep in front of your clients – but do make sure that they are appropriate to your clients' temperament or personality:
a. Drop off a proposal to them personally; or, if they're far away, add a special personal touch to the delivery.
b. Take the time to send them a handwritten thank-you note.
c. Send them a gift, such as flowers, on their birthday.
d. Again, follow through on all your promises to them.

 Deal with the challenge of cold calling.

Never has it been more difficult to call someone you don't know. You have to be aware of don't-call requests and more red tape that regulates whom you can call and when you can call them.

Follow the letter of the law, but do find a way to keep reaching out to new prospects. Remember how Tom reached out – with the alumni newsletter for his prospect "farm" from his high school. Plus, he turned a difficult task into the fun of catching up with his classmates and their parents.

You can produce newsletters; many firms can provide you with source material on your industry. Also, you can phone clients with the latest update or development that should matter to them. But get ready for some rejection. It comes with the territory. Don't take it personally and don't allow an abusive response to one of your inquiries to trigger inappropriate behavior on your part.

It helps to set a regular time for your cold calling. Also, do a quick inventory of your special gifts and talents to see what might help you break the ice with potential clients.

A word to the wise, though: Some old lines just don't work anymore. People have gotten much more sophisticated and much less patient when talking to strangers on the phone.

 Make those warm contacts.

Here's good news if you absolutely despise making cold calls. You can find success by cultivating your warm list of prospects. Start with the ones you already know, and then increase your universe of warm prospects by networking in your industry and community. After all, the ultimate goal of any successful sales professional is to establish a large and fruitful farm of warm prospects.

As we've mentioned, volunteer activities let you meet new individuals in your industry and your community in a more neutral and social setting. Another good way to build your warm farm is to obtain personal referrals from your existing warm list.

46 Spend your time with people who won't waste your time.

In real estate circles, we've all heard of the Looky-Lou, a seeming potential buyer who is either unwilling or unable to actually purchase a property. Other business settings have their Paper Tigers who act as if they have the authority to deal but don't. But the reality is the same for the sales people who encounter either: Usually a complete waste of time.

Some prospects require more time to close than others. For example, I called on a large bank for two years before the buyer gave me my first order. I had to spend more and more time with her and build up her trust in me until she had the confidence to give me a chance.

Conversely, try to identify real decision-makers in companies, families and other settings as soon as possible. Tom and I have heard war stories about salespeople who wasted hundreds of hours with clients who were not prepared or able to consummate the deal. When it happens to you, and it will, simply cut your losses and move on to the next qualified buyer.

Unfortunately, there is no way to categorically know someone is not going to deliver. So I advise my clients to set a limit in their minds in terms of time and energy. When they reach that limit, my clients find a professional way to either terminate their efforts or "close the deal." This latter option can be a delicate process; we'll discuss examples in later chapters that dissect the sales process.

47 Determine who the real players are and find a way to get their attention.

No matter how many billions are at stake in a given industry, it is quite easy to determine who the primary movers and shakers are and how to reach them. The hard part is finding a way to truly stand out to them. That's where your homework can help you. Many such people are in trade organizations, social causes or other groups, so volunteering might get you an introduction.

Sometimes you might only need to show up and tell them what you can do for them – your competitive advantages might be enough to get you in the door. There is no one answer or proven means, so it is up to you to get your foot in the door and find a way to sell.

Play the percentages and spend your time going after actual clients who will buy what you're selling. Find out who these decision-makers are and design the best plan to get you and what you're selling in front of them or someone they trust to screen for them. Once you get in the door with the client, close it to your competition by becoming indispensable to them.

At this point, your goal becomes having your client

become your promotional representative by telling friends about "this incredible supplier who has really made a difference for me!" Later we'll talk extensively about "word of mouth" referrals, the true gold standard for sales.

Things don't get any better than when your clients are referring you to their circle of friends.

Fall in love with people, not projects!

One reason to systematize your daily approach to your work is to give you an objective basis for evaluating your return on your investment of time, efforts and money. Above all, our approach to our jobs must always remain an objective and rational endeavor. When salespeople lose objectivity and begin to work for clients and projects for other more subjective reasons, there is a danger of investing tremendous amounts of time for little or no return on your investment.

Sometimes a project or property will have tremendous appeal for us. We might be tempted to spend more time, energy and resources because we feel like going all out. Be careful and stay objective. And to really assist your clients, prepare them for times when they might need to walk away from the table because the deal is not a good fit for them. It takes guts to keep your clients on track with their defined objectives when a deal is imminent – but if you believe the deal is not a good fit or doesn't make sense, whether for them or for your company, then walk away!

49 Sometimes the truth might hurt – but you must tell it!

Many times every day in our working lives, we need to know "the truth and nothing but the truth." The important thing is to face up to these situations and be strong enough to deliver that message. If you don't level with a client who is tolerating a situation that is hurting his business potential, the client could blame you when his numbers fall short.

When colleagues ask you for some honest input, give it to them. But be careful in the way you frame your assessment. You want to be sure that you're constructive and supportive. You need all of your tact to deliver the message and to make sure nothing you say is hurtful.

Also, we need to keep the communication channels open with all clients. Encourage them to let you know when they need something. If you don't exchange feedback constantly, your client might look elsewhere to find solutions for problems.

50 Get in your client's face!

Being in front of your client or prospect is the best way to build or strengthen a relationship. Selling is ALL about your relationships with your clients. We've won half the battle when clients begin to trust our assessments, our judgment and our promises to deliver for them. Obviously, it helps to spend as much quality time as possible with clients. Sometimes the best time with a client is actually time away from the office, when you can develop a sense of mutual respect for each other on a personal level.

If just one client is responsible for most of your business, it is imperative that you try to spend as much quality time as possible with that client. Literally, your business liveli-hood is at stake. You need to know when a competitor is attempting to move in on that business.

However, don't let insecurity drive anything you do to create face-to-face contact. Look for creative and innova-tive ways to stay in front of your client, but be careful not to become a pest!

 Master the art of appropriate gift giving for your clients.

Some clients appreciate a holiday gift or birthday celebra-tion. That is an effective way to show your appreciation for their business. If your client is a diehard sports fan and your firm has a corporate suite or box seats at your local stadium or arena, be sure to invite the client to a game.

But don't step over the line in showing appreciation for business. Tom used to get inappropriate requests from potential ad agency personnel for "referral fees" that amounted to kickbacks for help in getting key accounts. He politely declined.

You might hear stories about the different inappropriate ways your competitors acquire business accounts. But stay away from the temptation, because it can and will get you in real trouble. In most industries, it will even ruin your reputation in the long run. Most of us can see that this type of behavior is morally wrong. After all is said and done, you do have to look in the mirror from time to time!

52 Creating a newsletter will get you in front of potential clients.

We've already discussed how Tom transformed his cold calling into warm calling by using a "Where Are They Now?" column in his local real estate farm. This technique immediately reduced the resistance he faced, and the fact that he actually was a classmate of many of the sons and daughters of his prospects also helped him tremendously.

But even if you don't have a similar personal advantage to rely on, newsletters still provide substantial benefits. For instance, in rapidly appreciating markets for all industries, a newsletter can alert people to where the market is by including the latest sales information. This concept applies to financial news, too, such as the latest information on returns on types of investment.

Creating a newsletter (ideally, with assistance, research and resources from your firm) makes you an authority figure for the recipients. That gives you a perfect platform for gaining their respect and trust in the future. In the legal arena, online and printed newsletters can be invaluable in placing you in front of new prospects. If you are the leading authority on a given subject or area of practice, why not share that fact with as many potential and existing clients as possible?

If your newsletter is online – and that is a must nowadays – think about linking with other Web sites and online resources to maximize your reach. Also, be sure to keep your contact list as up-to-date as possible.

53   The power of word-of-mouth referrals.

Call us "old school," but both of us absolutely believe that this form of advertising and promotion is the most effective. The best way to describe word-of-mouth referrals from trusted and satisfied clients is "golden!"

No matter what the profession or industry, a word-of-mouth referral usually will get you the business. This is why our approach to writing this book is to lay a strong foundation for you. We advocate a systematic approach to how you render your services. We advise you to be attentive to details and to begin to anticipate your clients' needs to better serve them.

We believe it is more important for you to take a long-term view of your profession or industry – remember that advice about "a marathon, not a sprint." Take the time to "get it right," don't rush out and mismanage your initial clients and end up failing to serve them.

Think of this in terms of creating a pyramid. (No, not a pyramid scam or Ponzi scheme!) Our pyramid begins with our first client. It might have many peaks that represent subsequent clients as well. But our ability to build upon these peaks depends on how well we've satisfied the clients we're building upon. When they're totally satisfied, they usually become exuberant in assessing our services or products. Sometimes they ask us if we would mind them referring us to other potential clients – their friends!

Once, Tom dealt with Pat Cronin, a building contractor. Mr. Cronin, a true craftsman, treated his clients' homes with reverence. When he finished a remodeling job, he would review his work with the client, explaining the thought process behind the improvement (the "why" behind the work). When Tom reviewed the remodel work with Mr. Cronin, he was impressed not only with the final outcome but with all the thought and care that went into it.

As a result, Mr. Cronin worked with many of Tom's relatives and friends and they always thanked Tom for thinking enough of them to send Pat to them!

When exceptional professionals in sales or other fields give their clients exceptional service, the outcome can be incredible over time. Literally, such excellence can set into motion a tidal wave of referrals and positive goodwill for the fortunate firm that employs the "superstar" professional.

Enough said? Take the long view and work your tail off for every client. Of course, don't overextend and end up giving poor service to anyone. If you can't do the work, don't sign the client, because you can imagine the inverse of the examples above!

54 Strike while the iron is hot!

You can get an entire industry to discover you! One of the best ways is to trumpet your successes as soon as they occur, and afterwards, too. One of Tom's clients, the music composer Bryan Miller, composed music for three television commercials that were aired during the Super Bowl this year. Guess what Tom is doing now?

He's telling the advertising world about Bryan's accomplishment in a variety of forms in an integrated marketing campaign.

And when you do something truly amazing, perhaps on the scale of an attorney winning a big trial or forging a legal precedent, be extra-sure to tell your whole universe of potential clients about it.

But believe it or not, many professionals shy away from doing so. There might be reluctance to "toot your own horn" in industries such as finance or the law. But times have changed. Innovative and creative, yet dignified, solutions can communicate your "wins" to your potential client base.

Just look at Hollywood. Why do the major studios spend millions of dollars every year on promotional campaigns aimed at the voters for the entertainment industry's guild and festival honors, especially the Academy Awards?

The answer is two-fold but simple: Advertising works – and winning Oscars and other awards pays off at the box office.

So please apply this technique, appropriately and meaningfully. It will get you where you want to go in your profession or industry!

 Know what they expect of you in your new sales career.

If you're a recent college graduate deciding between job offers, take the time to get all of the facts from your prospective employers. The best job interviews should facilitate two-way communication between the parties. No one wants to see you depart after a few frustrating weeks or months on the job because you "really were not cut out for the demands" of the job.

If you already have a job in one field and are considering shifting into a new line of work, you also need to do some research and some soul-searching. One of my friends switched from corporate sales to real estate and was surprised to discover how many phone calls she received and how much attention the clients needed. This was very different from the servicing required in her corporate job.

Different businesses require different styles, hours, personalities and responsibilities to obtain clients and to keep those clients satisfied.

 Process your data.

Sometimes my clients fall into complacency because they have all the latest gadgets, from PDA's to cell phones. But even with all of the resources that are at our disposal, I often find people wasting precious prime selling time to search for a piece of paper with a new prospect's phone number or e-mail address.

Is your desk completely organized and neat? Many of us let our desktops become cluttered with paperwork that includes old mail, receipts, client folders, checkbooks, CD's and diskettes, etc.

Sound familiar?

If you want a stopgap measure to help you sort through this chaos, buy some average paper tablets like your kids use in school – the best ones are big (8.5 x 11 inches). Just open the cover up and start with the first page. For a week, write down all your phone notes and other information in the tablet.

At the end of the week, if you've proceeded sequentially, you'll have all your notes in one place. You won't have any more panic attacks – because you'll know where your data is.

Naturally, the better way to go is to use one of the recommended sales software programs. Log your client information directly into that program as you receive it. However, human beings often don't do what is best for them. Many of us still haven't figured out how to completely use our new cell phones, let alone the old VCR players that are still locked on 12:00 at home.

So use your paper tablet and stop using the backs of those unopened mail envelopes on your desk to record the important follow-up data you'll be needing, say, to close a sale in the next few days. Notebooks are simple, and there is still something to be said for the old "K.I.S.S." method!

Make the telephone your friend!

Bear with us here; we know this focus point sounds really basic. But do you know how many reputable companies FAIL to call back potential clients? Example: Tom recently tried to hire a roofing company that the local roofing supply firm recommended highly. Tom left a message, but the roofing company never returned the call! That is inexcusable: This company alienated a potential client. It also narrowly escaped sending a red flag to the firm that recommended it, which a complaint by Tom would have triggered.

While we're on this subject, how is your phone system serving you now?

When someone calls you or your company, does a human being answer the phone? Or do you subject your potential clients to frustrating phone systems that drive them crazy? When you're in your office and the phone rings, answer it! Don't drive your potential clients away because you don't want to interrupt your work of the moment.

We're talking about those answering systems that have the caller opt for a given individual before routing the call to voice mail. If you're in, why not just pick up, or at least pick up when the caller designates you?

If you can afford to hire a receptionist to answer your phones, make sure you train her well. When potential clients call, she is the one who represents your company. Yes, such training is one more task for someone with your company. But it is critical that your receptionist and anyone else who answers the phone have a professional demeanor and provide valuable assistance to callers.

58 What have you done for your clients lately?

Always remember that in the final analysis, what truly impresses your clients is your performance. As we've said, it helps a sales professional to dress well and drive a luxury car. But over the long haul, everyone in sales needs to stay focused on the question, "What have I done for my clients lately?" Believe me, that's what the clients are thinking!

59 Develop a sales approach to buyers that WORKS.

Fortunately, there are classic works on selling that you can mine, and we'll give you "Sales 101" and "Long-Term Relationships and Networking" in later chapters. And at the end of this book you'll find "Leslie's Library," which lists a few of my personal favorites.

You need to become an expert at overcoming objections, closing a sale, strategic selling, business development (soft sales), planning and goal-setting. You also need to follow through with action steps. We include all these ideas in this book.

Obviously, buyers need to trust their representatives and the information and assessments they supply. This usually means that if you are a representative, you have a fiduciary relationship to buyers that requires you to act in their best interest as they express it to you.

This is pretty serious stuff. It's not about life and death, but it is about economic well-being. Always remember that your buyer is looking to you as an authority on any given transaction. None of us is perfect, and often we can't predict negative outcomes despite our best efforts. But you need to ask yourself questions. Have you given your buyers your best effort? Have you lived up to their expectations? Have you lived up to your own expectations, which should be even higher?

Despite the constant pressure that all of us face to meet and exceed our sales volume quotas, we also must deliver the highest value possible to our clients. For real estate buyers in today's bull markets in hot sectors such as Southern California, our agent or broker might be doing a great job of giving us the small edge that gets us the property we want in a multiple-offer scenario.

Sometimes in such cases, an agent or broker will find a time advantage for presenting the client's offer before the flood of additional offers pours in. Or an agent or broker can do something subtle, such as increasing the amount of the buyer's good faith deposit for the offer from something minimal ($2,000) to something a little more substantial ($5,000-10,000), and that ends up making the difference in getting the buyer that property!

It is a difficult process, but no one said it would be easy. You need to study from the masters and apply their techniques to your work with your buyers. You need to actually deliver on your buyer's expectations and your own.

You also need to have a thorough mastery of your sales practice so you can provide the highest degree of business intelligence to your buyers. This is an especially important point for financial and legal professionals, because that's why their clients are coming to them in the first place.

Finally, in the heat of battle, you need to be able to make the difference for your clients and get them the property or results they seek.

So don't be afraid of becoming a sales "super-hero," because that is what our profession requires!

60 Develop a sales approach to sellers that WORKS.

Virtually everything we've just said about working with buyers applies to this focus point as well. However, there is a difference in psychology. In working with sellers, we need to show ourselves in an even more credible light. We also need time to build trust with the seller.

In real estate, if you represent a motivated buyer who will go the distance to acquire a property, the transaction probably will be fairly simple and easy for you. But to be able to list a property, you need to be someone whom the seller trusts and values.

Fortunately, being associated with a trusted real estate firm that has deep ties to the community will help you get listings. Sellers often have pre-existing relationships with their brokers and agents as well. After all, who handled their transaction when they were buying their properties? If sales professionals have taken care of business, they will still be in the picture when the time comes for the sellers to list the subject property. Things just seem to get a little more complicated when it comes to getting the listings.

Also, when you are working with the seller, the ultimate objective becomes maximizing the seller's return from the transaction. This can create some problems in today's crazy markets.

If prices are climbing in a frenzied real estate market, the listing agent or broker will want to set an asking price that reflects what's going on in that location but that also allows for more appreciation and the best possible offer prices. However, if the price is set too high, the seller may seem greedy or unrealistic. In that case, local agents and brokers might back away from the property.

61 To get new business, use all your ammunition to sell your client.

Get a good opportunity to make your case in front of the key decision-maker. This is the time to mention your qualifications and track record, as well as your firm's track record in the industry if it will help. It's also the time to identify all the primary benefits your client will get from working with you. If your company is small, you'll talk about personal service and commitment. If your company is large, you'll talk about client savings that result from all the business your firm books.

You'll want to include your own primary strengths, too, because you'll be the key client liaison. In some respects, you'll also represent the client's interests in given situations. Depending on the size of this account, you can even borrow a page from the advertising world and do some client work on speculation, just to demonstrate the strength of your marketing skill. Be careful with this one, however, because it might be hard to keep those trade secrets of yours if the client selects another firm.

Make sure you take proper advantage of your personal strengths in all phases of your client service (before, during and in the evaluation stages). If you happen to be a strong writer, generate integrated communications to take advantage of that strength.

This can include thoughtful and well-written prospecting letters that also contain recent successes, all the way to detailed proposals that document the depth of your marketing services and intelligence. If your strength is in verbal communication, you'll want to make your strongest case face-to-face with your prospects.

That's why when you're starting out it's critical to do homework on yourself as well as your potential prospects. You need to build the strongest case you can for your product or services. You also need to go to your strengths to win and make the difference in highly competitive situations.

An important note: When for some reason you don't get the account, try to learn from that setback. As we've indicated above, most business professionals believe they've learned the most from their failures, not their successes. But in this process it's important to be completely honest and objective.

Sometimes, sales people realize they could have gotten the business if the company hadn't dropped the ball. Of course, if this happens very often, sales people go to a firm that will advance their efforts, not hinder them.

Before you abandon the sales process, make sure you've done everything you could to win the business. Don't look back and wish you'd made one more follow-up call or been more available to a client during the discussion phase.

62 Keep your management people in the loop.

Keeping leadership up to date on your activities gives you credibility and enables them to assist you in the sales process. Over the years, I acquired invaluable tools and insights from my sales management. Often, it takes some extra effort to copy them on important client-related activities. But it will be worth your time in terms of the outcome ($$$$).

You never know: Your manager might have just the right advice for you because he or she probably was in your shoes before becoming a sales manager. We believe in taking advantage of all resources at your disposal, and your manager is your first line of support.

63 Stay in communication with your clients.

Stay connected with your clients. Even when nothing has happened and there is no apparent reason to call, you still want to keep the existing relationship strong. Don't waste your clients' time, but do find creative ways to keep updating them. Perhaps you can suggest a schedule revision or offer another relevant idea. Stay in touch with these very important people!

64 "Network...network...network!"

Make an effort to get to know and build quality relationships with the key movers and shakers in your industry and community. If you do some homework, you will know who they are and which industry and community groups they patronize.

Bankers, attorneys, accountants and other key executives who serve many clients can be invaluable to you as sources of introductions to key prospects you want to reach. That kind of introduction will immediately turn a "cold call" into a much warmer one. And often, just-introduced new contacts can then introduce you to still more people.

Attending industry trade shows is a must, because you'll get the chance to meet all the major players in your field. Depending on what your industry is, many of your clients might be there, too. Attend trade shows, too, because they deal with the issues that will challenge your industry. You need to stay on the leading edge of such developments and concerns.

This focus point on networking is just as significant as the adage in real estate: "Location...location...location!"

 To supplement your skills, hire the experts you need.

This focus point goes hand in hand with the previous one, because it can make your networking more effective. Naturally, none of us is good at everything. So we need to acknowledge our limitations and be willing to deal with them. We can "fill in the blanks" with outside consultants and services for areas such as finance, coaching, letter-writing, time management, organization, planning, physical conditioning and therapy.

Once you've brought experts onto your team, always treat them with respect and loyalty. Not only do they deserve it, they might become valuable members of your network

 Specialize in your industry as soon as possible.

From "Day One," make a special effort to develop expertise in a valuable niche in your industry or community. When you become a leading authority on a subject, your potential clients will come to you because they'll want the best counsel they can receive.

In real estate, this niche can be a category in the marketplace, such as a certain type of investment properties or a type of investment. Your expertise can also apply to a given territory, and your goal could be to become the dominant agent or broker in that territory.

We all love to work with the "Number One" anything in our daily lives. Tom did that last year while buying a new car. First, he made sure that he was dealing with the leading sales agent in the office. He also did the deal on the last day of the month, and the office happened to be just behind on its sales quota. So his agent had maximum leverage because she was "Number One," his bid had maximum impact because of the timing – and Tom got a great deal!

So much information is at our fingertips on the Internet that we have unlimited opportunity to acquire the latest data on prices, trends and everything else going on in our neck of the woods. And when things get a little complicated many industry classes and seminars are available to help you with what you'd like to learn.

Once you've acquired your expertise and your sales niche, integrate these "badges of distinction" into all your marketing and promotional efforts. By the way, one excellent source of business for sales professionals is public speaking opportunities at business or industry functions and conferences for professionals such as lawyers and financial experts. At your earliest opportunity, find forums for presentations and attend seminars on public speaking. It will serve you well, but it is an art you need to practice and refine before you can become truly effective.

67 Be responsive to your client's requests for help and information.

In today's competitive world, we need to respond promptly and efficiently when clients need help and information. Some clients seem to need constant attention – but if we're using a systematic approach to our work and tracking our respective rates of profitability for each client, we'll already know who is providing us or our firm with the greatest return on our investment of time.

In other words, when our "Number One" client calls, we need to be on our toes. If we're not, one of our competitors will be glad to do the job! Also, look on the bright side when a newer client calls. It's one more chance to build a strong relationship with that client.

68 Take pride in your profession and your industry.

I'm currently doing sales seminars for a major financial firm's regional offices. It is a source of pride for all sales professionals to see that the financial and legal communities now completely embrace marketing and business development programs.

Another source of pride for sales people involves maximizing sales and marketing opportunities. Income is a primary accomplishment in all industries, including ours, of course; and we all can take satisfaction in knowing that many leading sales professionals earn mid-six-figure incomes. At my most recent thank-you luncheon for my client base and networking group, many heavy hitters attended. So many, in fact, that I said the sales people present probably were responsible for about 25% of the print jobs in Southern California that year!

While on this topic, I want to make an important point about why we do what we do in our profession. A few years ago, I attended a "Lifetime Achievement Night for Max Goodrich," a sales legend in the printing industry. At the podium that night, he said how honored he was to have had the privilege of serving his clients and his firm. He confided that this was what mattered most to him.

Now, obviously, we all need money – to make a living, support our families, meet our financial obligations, save for the future and fulfill our job requirements. But in an age that seems fixated on making more money all the time, it's nice to know that for Max Goodrich, an all-time sales great, money was a by-product of his deep commitment to serve his fellow man. Let's try to remember this as we go about our service to our clients and our firms.

69   Be proud of your company and associate with the "best of the best."

Never take your firm for granted. Often, companies have long and illustrious histories. They've paved the way for many of today's breakthroughs and products. We also know that many leading industries require tremendous capital investment, and that owners and management often deal with gut-wrenching financial issues, yet somehow they manage to keep the lights on and keep their services and resources available to us when we need support.

My career has enabled me to gain insight from just about every vantage point in many different industries. As a result, I encourage all of my sales associates to demonstrate their pride and loyalty in their firms and on behalf of their client base.

Also, when you do have the chance to get to know a sales pro in your industry, see if that person might be interested in becoming a mentor for you. Often, such individuals derive a great deal of satisfaction from helping one of the "young pups" in the office. The most important thing you need to show such a person is your desire to master the craft of selling and to acknowledge that you don't quite know it all yet.

 Don't sweat the small stuff.

We've all had people in our office who seem to get worked up and testy about almost anything. Most successful people don't have time for such foolishness. They've learned to focus their energies on what they can control and change, and not to let the little things get to them.

When you're new in an office situation, it's really important to give yourself a chance to pick up on the ebb and flow of that business environment so you look like you know what you're doing (at least some of the time!). A tip: Find a friendly and knowledgeable person during your first week to give you the "lay of the land" so you can fit in and make your mark by simply selling. Don't get flustered over trifles. Try not to be noticed too much until you really have a sense of how to handle yourself in this new environment. Just apply lessons you learned in your previous job and school situations, and adapt!

This challenge is another reason to consider doing an internship while you're still in school. That way, you can learn things in a relatively low-pressure setting – because no one expects much from an intern in the first place. So when you surprise them with your wonderful qualities and valuable talents and skills, you might just be getting an inside path to your first job after you graduate!

Lastly, by gaining a perspective on things and knowing when to assert yourself, you'll be ready to meet life's challenges.

 Don't forget to bring your sense of humor with you!

Having a sense of humor can really help you cope with the stress of creating your vision and implementing your plan to get the ball rolling. Being able to laugh at ourselves while on our journey is a key to growth. It also helps us be more persistent. We need to keep a positive perspective as much as possible and not let disappointments and discouragement defeat us.

 See the big picture by staying well informed on current events.

Our world has never been so interdependent. It makes sense to keep yourself informed about current events and other major developments. If you develop a "tunnel view" that is concerned only with the latest news in your industry, you'll miss out on other sales opportunities and important trends that will affect your industry.

Also, won't you feel more comfortable at your next social event if you know just a little bit about the latest big story everyone is talking about? An excellent source for the big picture, and of course for breaking business news, is the Wall Street Journal. I recommend the Journal, plus specific industry trade publications, to all my coaching clients.

73 | Engage in competitive analysis, a constant requirement to keep your edge!

Knowing what the competition is up to is invaluable. This means knowing about every benefit and feature that anyone is offering in the battle for sales. When you are formulating your sales and marketing plan, take the time to find out what the industry leaders are doing. Go to their web sites and review their promotional materials. See who their clients are and what they are doing for them.

Your competitors are not going to send you their materials. But if you have a supportive network of friends, they can help keep you up to speed on what the competition is doing to get ahead and stay ahead. This process can be as simple as reading your industry trades and reviewing the competing ads.

Make sure your firm and your services get listed on all the "free" links and other resource information transmitted within your industry. Usually, there is a "hot" newsletter in the industry that most of the leading clients subscribe to and read; make sure that publication profiles your company and your services.

Even in these times of continual technological breakthroughs, most of the techniques for making sales are tried and true and do not change. As we know, the techniques that get us face-to-face with potential clients are the best ones, because that personal connection can drive their business to us.

In real estate, listing agents provide competitive property analysis and project potential sales prices, hoping to acquire a listing. Other brokers and agents send periodical newsletters with tips and recent sales prices in the neighborhood.

To expedite sales, many real estate offices now tape tours of their sellers' properties or offer web-related access or services to find qualified buyers. In other industries, firms constantly try to "one up" the competition by developing clever marketing slogans that differentiate themselves through superior advertising ideas. This is the basis for consumer advertising campaigns that often spend millions of dollars to create product awareness and drive purchasing.

Industries that involve high finance, investments or legal services put more of a premium on knowledge, expertise and communication. A client will want the best counsel for every business contact or transaction. However, we still must know what the competition is up to – to counter any initiatives they try with our clients.

Become aware of the tone your competition is using to reach its potential client base. Learn as much as possible about using the best and most appropriate graphic design and advertising aesthetic to describe your services. This is especially vital for professionals such as lawyers, accountants and management consultants.

74 Remember, this is a marathon and not a sprint.

I know you're determined to stand out immediately from the rest of the pack and to make your mark in your industry. That's good, but be careful not to fall into a trap. Achieving true success in an industry can take some time. You need to prepare yourself for the long haul in pursuing career growth, building your business and attracting new clients who will help you get where you want to go.

I encourage my clients to take many small steps that lead to where they want to go.

See this endeavor as a journey that is not overnight but consists of "doable" components. That will help you develop qualities useful for the entire journey.

Continual positive steps bring us closer and closer to our expressed objectives. One such step is to include physical exercise – say, long-distance running or regular workouts at the club – to build up not only your body but also your sense of discipline in pursuit of a goal.

75 Have an ultimate "to do" list.

Tom credits college football coach Lou Holtz with making him aware of the utility of having an ambitious "goals list" of things you want to accomplish in your life. Holtz created a list of 107 lifetime goals and at last count had reached 99 of them.

Often, it is extremely helpful to focus on specific goals (remember Susan's new kitchen in Chapter Two?). Compile a master list of goals, and as you accomplish each one, put a check mark by it and move on to another item. I will share one of my goals with you: I want to scuba dive in Australia on the Great Barrier Reef

The act of writing something down furthers your awareness of it and makes it more likely that you will actually do it. Somehow, this act makes us just a little more accountable for the outcome. I always encourage my clients to commit their objectives to written expression.

In my coaching sessions, my clients also write down the weekly "homework" they've agreed to accomplish between sessions. Committing goals to writing also allows us to measure our progress and to make any changes needed for success.

You can devise a cumulative "wish list" yourself, of course, but you might also want to create it in cooperation with your spouse, boyfriend or girlfriend – out of fairness and because that person will play a large part in your ability to reach your goals.

76 Always seek feedback on how well you are doing with your clients.

This is one of the most difficult things to do – and one of the most necessary. From time to time, we all have less-than-perfect experiences with clients. The communication process can become flawed or the client's expectations can be just a little bit unrealistic.

No matter what goes wrong with a client, we still need to have the fortitude to offer to fix it. However, if the primary problem is with the client, you might need to move on to other prospects. That depends on the contributions of the client to your firm's bottom line. Most of us have dealt with someone who can be characterized as "the client from hell," whom nothing will ever satisfy.

Unless a client like that is the one keeping your firm's doors open and lights burning, you might want to graciously remove yourself from further humiliation and frustration. Life is too short to go through hell for a difficult, demanding client who just doesn't get it. I would rather lose that client than half my sales staff in the process!

Fortunately, most clients are not like that. They simply need to know that we want their constant feedback on how we're doing for them. You might learn something about your style or personality that you're not even aware of, and it might help you in the long run. Also, it is much better for your clients to know they can talk to you about a problem area and that you will respond to their concerns.

It does take a pretty competent and confident individual to adopt this policy with clients, though. Sometimes we might not want to hear what they say. However, if your firm's policy is not to assign blame but to focus on fixing what is amiss, everyone will benefit.

To incorporate such a policy, a firm can appoint an independent third party to elicit comments from clients. They could be reluctant to open up to their normal liaison if something about that person is part of the problem. But again, when everyone buys in to the concept of providing exceptional service to the firm's clients, and when the process is a positive one and not an internal blame game, then everyone will benefit.

 77 Build on a solid foundation of excellence when you're starting out.

This focus point is invaluable if applied. In the beginning of your career, it is vital to build a solid foundation in your approach to building the business. Find mentors who manifest a "best practices" mentality and who are truly role models for you.

Also, you'll need to find a way to put in the time that is necessary at this stage of your development. As we've discussed before, you'll never stand out from the pack if you have a "9-to-5" approach to your career. You'll need to get to the office early and be prepared to be the last one to leave. Because you are the "new rep" in the office, everything will be new to you and things will take longer to fall into place.

But once you absorb these lessons, you should be set to apply them from then on and you can move on to learning something else. A mentor who has a proven "track record" in the industry can alert you to specific problem areas and help you to model the productive things they do that contribute to their success.

To get to know these special achievers, you'll need to commit to attending sales seminars and training seminars within your firm and in your industry. Sometimes an expert who is teaching a seminar will be impressed that you are there and that you care enough to want to be the best that you can be.

As I tell my clients, if you really "want it," you will find a way to succeed by exhausting every reasonable and ethical means of advancing in your industry!

78 | Be the one to "push the envelope" in your industry!

In every area of practice, you can find examples of innovative ideas and campaigns that have succeeded in your locale or elsewhere. One way to innovate in your community is to be aware of success stories and case studies in other areas. You can model that success by being willing to incorporate approaches from other places.

Start to brainstorm creatively, either alone or with others similarly inclined. You just might come up with a brilliant idea to implement for yourself or your firm. Sometimes a simple observation can spark an idea that becomes the basis for an entire sales or marketing idea or campaign

Innovation can result in breakthroughs in sales prospecting techniques, customer service strategies and solution selling programs. Just keep your eyes open and observe what seems to be working around you. You never know when you might come up with a million-dollar idea!

79 Know where to draw the line with your challenging clients.

If our firm or enterprise is relatively healthy and prospering, we will be able from time to time to take a radical step that most of us relish: If a client has crossed the line from "difficult and demanding" to "too difficult and too demanding," we can decide to cease rendering services for that client.

The sun will rise the next day, and the stars will not fall from the sky because of this reasoned decision. In fact, there might be those who actually admire such an action, and our drawing a line in the sand will reinforce our dealings with other borderline clients.

However, at all times we need to be careful to correctly characterize our clients' conduct. It is human nature for people to become frustrated by circumstances on occasion.

We need to be aware of all of the facts and stay in constant communication with our clients to find out what is happening with them. We tend to forget that they are beset with as many challenges and obstacles in their daily governance as we are.

At a difficult time, valued clients need to know you are there for them. Such loyalty and special attention might earn you their prolonged business and deep respect. I have known a number of talented clients who required the best of my services because they had numbers to meet and pressures to face. I never regret having provided the greatest degree of service that I could muster. They rewarded my efforts with their business patronage and their respect and friendship.

80 Think about team selling!

It's here and it's only getting bigger! Team selling uses the same accountability principles that I use in my coaching practice. When you commit to an objective or a task, your teammate is counting on you to follow through. Also, all of us have a number of strengths and weaknesses. Wouldn't it be great to find a teammate and sales partner whose strengths are your weaknesses and whose weaknesses are your strengths?

However, be careful that your teammate is not just along for the ride off your efforts or unique talents and skills. This is one of the most important decisions that you will make, so I suggest that you take a little time to get to know your associates before rushing off to the field as the newest team in the office.

You will need to employ the same keen observational skills that you used for finding your mentor. Don't rush in; wait to team up with a partner who will truly complement your efforts.

"Fuel for
Our Journey"

The following focus points provide us with the fuel we'll need to keep running this marathon that will determine the outcome of our business careers.

 Get your three "squares" each day.

Take a step back every once in a while to get a proper perspective on your progress. Make sure you're getting – and giving – everything you need to attain the success you desire. Take inventory to see if you have the tools at hand to stay motivated. Consider the level of support you're receiving on the job and at home. What needs to change to get you where you need to be? Are you staying balanced with plenty of exercise? Are you making the time to stay informed about all the new developments in your industry?

Early on, you can set up your own motivational library at home. It should consist of videos and books from inspirational authors both within the sales and marketing areas but also from the outside world. When you find yourself in need of a quick "pick me up," watch an inspirational movie. You can't afford to allow yourself to function for very long at an average or sub-par level. You, and probably your sales manager, will know when that is occurring. So fix it before it's too late and you're out the door!

82 | Get "nutrition" from varied activities.

My sister once told me, "Fill up your bean jar." What she meant was that I needed to keep my batteries charged by taking in "nutrients" from activities such as a good workout or hike, lunch with a good friend, attendance at a worship service or reading a great book. She wanted me to find people, places or things that would re-charge and energize me for my next client, job, adventure or difficult assignment.

Those of us who have families can view our familial responsibilities as opportunities for this type of recharging. Just look into those big beautiful eyes of your child, if you are so blessed; there is your joy for this moment!

83 | Be a lean, mean, "fighting machine!"

Be a sales warrior when you walk into that office, pick up that phone or make that presentation. Don't let anything else distract you or take away from your mission to be the best sales professional that you can be.

Believe me, I have heard it all when it comes to excuses for poor results. Often, the excuses relate to baggage that the individual is still carrying around because of pre-existing problems such as a previous relationship or a continuing credit or financial problem.

When we decide to become sales professionals, we need to shed any baggage from the past that is hurting our current performance. We simply can't afford to let an old hang-up hold us back. Some might have problems with trusting, because of past events. Others might have lingering financial concerns; we might even be maxed out on our credit cards or in danger of being evicted.

If this is the case, get your financial affairs in order before you undertake a career that compensates you based primarily on your performance. If you're just starting out as a salesperson and your income will be based mostly upon your sales commissions, you need to have a substantial cushion in place before you start selling. Often, there is a substantial lead-time to your first few sales and you need to be prepared for that initial learning curve.

That's where the "lean and mean" stuff comes into play. In the early stages, watch carefully what's going out of your account, so you'll be able to hang in there for the long haul! Don't commit to that $60K luxury car quite yet until you know if you have what it takes to finish this marathon!

 Dine out often.

We have already discussed the importance of maintaining "face time" with your clients. When you're starting out and attempting to build your sales practice, meals will provide you with an excellent means of reaching all of the key principals who need to be part of your sales team.

When Tom was establishing his sports marketing practice, he had more than 50 lunches with individuals who were already established in this industry. He did his homework so he knew as much as possible about the individual he was inviting to lunch. After a few minutes, Tom's enthusiasm for the sports marketing industry would become apparent and the individual would begin to "talk turkey" about potential avenues for mutual gain. It was a lot of work, but this process helped establish his firm and led to his first couple of clients.

There is just something about breaking bread with some-one that is a good thing. That's why I continue to utilize lunch or dinner (if applicable) as a primary method of spending time with my best clients or potential clients. And I always pick up the tab!

85 | Keep up to speed on the latest business tools.

If you're not technologically savvy, find someone who can help you wade through the sea of new devices such as PDA's, sales lead and data management software and any other valuable Web-related resources that can improve your organization skills and help you make that sale! It's truly amazing how quickly some of these items become standard issue in our businesses. Can you imagine what a client would think of you if you didn't use a cell phone or pager? Make sure you're on the front end of this business tool curve and not lagging in the back. This is especially important for the sales veterans who might resist some current tools. Perception is still very important, and you don't want to be thought of as a dinosaur who is lagging behind the latest developments.

One nice benefit of business tools is the speed in which you have access to the latest information. Believe me, clients will be impressed by such capabilities and you'll give them the impression that you're on top of your game. Hopefully, they will feel that way after the transaction or sale as well.

86 Reward yourself on a regular basis.

When all is said and done, we do want to receive some enjoyment from life while we're carving out our niche in our industries. In the early days of my sales career, one of my mentors shared with me how she stopped at a little place each day for a small snack or treat to reward herself for a job well done that day.

Obviously, you can expand upon this concept and make your treat a little larger. Remember the example of my client Susan, who wanted to attain a new kitchen and placed the picture in her office area to remind herself of that objective? You could take the vacation that you and your family have been planning, or you can buy yourself a special gift you've been wanting.

But the important thing is to take care of yourself and not just your clients in this lifetime. If we lose that sense of ourselves and our days are only filled with tasks we need to do, and with deadlines (such as quotas) that we need to meet, we won't maintain our balance or motivation for very long.

So remember to incorporate the power of the reward into your daily efforts.

Stay up when you're selling!

The next time you close a big deal you've been working on for a while, take a moment to think of every other potential client or deal that could be addressed as well.

What am I getting at here? Simply this: The best time to sell is right after we get "a win," because making that sale gives our confidence a big lift and we feel as if we're suddenly on top of the world.

When we feel like this, we want to maximize the potential results. So postpone the celebration for one day. Take advantage of the momentum and "edge" you now have, and get out there and close those other deals!

88 Celebrate your wins.

After you've continued to work through the immediate "afterglow" of your "win," do take some time to celebrate. Also, when you break through and become a member of a higher sales level club, pat yourself on the back and find a meaningful way to reward yourself for the accomplishment.

These "wins" are the outcome that we work to achieve. When we get them, we need to enjoy the moment and add that luster to our lives. However, there are certain individuals who don't take this approach. Everyone is unique, so if something works for you, go with it!

89 | Have a buddy!

Whether it's a family member or your best friend, you need to have a buddy you can confide in when you need to talk to someone. It's a two-way street; you can be a good listener for your buddy as well. We all need to be able to deal with things and get them off our chest so we can keep going!

It's also a good idea to have a sales buddy. If you're part of a two-person sales team, it might be our partner. But sometimes, we'll select someone for that role whom we're not working with every day. You'll know the person who is best for this in your office when you find him or her.

90 | Share the load!

A great way to off-load some of the natural pressure you're dealing with is to engage the services of a qualified sales or corporate coach. This can lighten your load so you can focus on important selling tasks and client-related action items. Also, because many of us are working out of our homes or functioning as sole proprietors, we can often use this regular interaction to keep us on track and committed to our business success.

This kind of "teaming" can also bring two points of view into the equation when focusing on a specific problem or concern. Often, gaining an additional perspective will make all the difference!

91 Finding the right coach for you.

Because coaching is a growing field and exists in most sales professions, you can begin by contacting coaches who are working with your most successful associates. Next, you can make inquiries by contacting the most successful sales professionals in your industry.

When you get the chance to meet your prospective coach, remember that this is a two-way street. You'll need to interview the coaching candidate as well as to provide information for your candidate to consider. What is the coach's experience level? Sales background, if any? Educational background? Do your personalities appear to mesh? Does your coach have references from other successful clients that are relevant to your professional objectives? What does your "gut" tell you about this coach? I often encourage my clients to trust their intuitive feelings in given situations, and this is one of them.

92 Give your coach your total "buy-in."

Once you're confident that you have the coach you want, take the next most important step in assuring the success of this endeavor: Do your part to make it successful.

During your sessions, mention your objectives for the program. When your coach gives you homework to do before the next session, give it the attention it deserves. Unfortunately, some people never make a complete commitment to their coaches. They hold back important information or they view the process as something foisted upon them by their sales managers.

If that's the case, the coach will know it. In time, a coach might decide you're not worth the effort – and might stop working with you. Your lack of effort could discourage a coach and dim his or her view of your prospects.

When I determine that a client hasn't *bought in* to the program we've mutually determined, I have a heart-to-heart and offer the client one more opportunity to commit. Naturally, I realize that circumstances sometimes are beyond a client's control. I do accommodate situations such as when a successful business deal drains a client's time – because facilitating my clients' success is the very essence of the coaching relationship.

But when the client simply isn't up for our program, it's better for all concerned for the coach to end the relationship. Fortunately, the vast majority of my clients go "above and beyond" the requirements, and their outcomes are positive!

Translate your passion into your occupation!

This book primarily is for sales professionals and everyone who wants to incorporate sales and business development principles into their business careers. What if you're taking your first steps in the business world and trying to decide what you really want to do for a living?

If you recall, at the beginning of this book we spent a lot

of time on the importance of you determining your dream and finding the strength to pursue it.

This is one of the most important things we can do in our lives and in our careers! Let's face it, some of us have dreams that involve long odds, and probably our family or friends have discouraged us from pursuing those dreams.

Perhaps you want to become a makeup artist or a singer or actor? Those pursuits are extremely difficult to attain, and they all involve substantial risk of failure. But, who knows? You could be the next sensation. Sometimes, it's better to take your chances initially and see if you can make your dreams come true!

For example, Tom has worked for more than 20 years with hundreds of individuals who dream of making the U.S.A. Olympic Team. That's one of the most difficult objectives imaginable, considering that you need to be the best in your given event for our entire nation!

Add to this the fact that usually you need to train for up to four years just for the chance to try to make the team, and you have a seemingly impossible and incredibly difficult undertaking. That's why Tom so highly admires every American Olympian and every hopeful who even tries to make the Olympic team.

Why not decide to go for your dreams as soon as possible after you've completed your educational program? For most of us, completing our undergraduate and post-graduate studies is a pretty good idea. It will provide us with a number of options for the future, and we'll have something to fall back on if our dream doesn't work out exactly as we'd hoped.

Besides, if your dream is something that does translate into a business career, your education will greatly improve your chances of success!

94 | Know when to say, "Enough is enough."

Sometimes people pursue a dream or career that turns out not to be right for them. Perhaps we've imagined becoming the next "American Idol" or "Star Search" champion. That dream is a long shot from the start, just because of the high number of competitors who see themselves in the same role. And it'll soon become "the impossible dream" for any hopeful who can't sing well!

This can happen in sales, too. Sometimes, no matter how badly people want a particular profession, the truth is that they're really cut out for another one. They might be too conscientious, always looking for the perfect property or transaction that rarely comes along. They simply might not be "people persons" and can't relate to most buyers, sellers or clients.

Or perhaps, they're pursuing a sales career, or another career that doesn't suit their strengths or personality, only because their role models were in those professions. In any case, before you decide to "reach for the stars," do your homework and really find out what the requirements for success are in the endeavor you're considering.

Also, you might want to incorporate Tom's 80/20 rule, to some degree, so you can improve your odds for ultimate success. Remember, Tom spends 80% of his time focused on his "meat and potatoes" – his business affairs and marketing practice with clients – and just 20% on projects and ventures that could have a higher degree of financial return but are only speculative.

That way, Tom safely maintains his profit stream so he can meet all his obligations, but he also gives his firm the opportunity to greatly enhance its bottom line when any of the more speculative ventures succeed.

If you take the time to study successful actors and recording artists, you'll find that many of them had to deal with failure early in their careers, but that success came to the ones who persisted, made the necessary changes and adjustments and stayed in the business!

95 Overcome the bumps in the road!

Have you known people who had a primary personality characteristic that seemed to hold them back in their lives? For instance, the know-it-alls who just have to let everyone know they've got the answer for everything in life. They might be perfectly suited to win a fortune on a game show that rewards such behavior, but most of us really don't appreciate being around them!

What about people who can never make up their mind? Their inability to commit to a decision or course of action can paralyze them. Then there are the perpetual students, who seem to want to avoid ever having to actually make a living. They take such an endless stream of classes that they wind up staying in college for even twice as long as necessary.

Most of us don't fall into these personality types. But we will encounter things along the way that can throw us off stride, such as temporary financial difficulties, a relationship that harms us and our self-esteem, or involvement in litigation or disputes over a client or transaction.

It's essential not to let your focus get stuck in the past, on some difficulty. You must maintain a positive frame of mind; you must keep moving forward in your life. Even something that might seem to be "the end of the world" will often end up being resolved.

None of us can focus all our energy on the bumps in the road. Do your best to learn to roll with the punches; that way, you'll become mentally tougher. Surround yourself with people who'll be there for you and who'll provide the counsel and wisdom you need when the going does get tough!

96 Let go of those who keep holding you back.

You probably already know who they are; for example, a boyfriend or girlfriend who constantly undermines your ability to achieve your legitimate objectives. That is a wrenching problem. Can you find a way to come to mutual accommodation? If not, you might need to decide what is more important to you: this person in your life, or your ability to succeed in your chosen career.

When Tom attended evening law school, the students in the program were advised that their four-year commitment would require a great deal of sacrifice and would need support from spouses and significant others. Tragically, by the time graduation came four years later, nearly a third of the married students were in various stages of splitting up!

Obviously, there often is a chance that we can deal effectively with any and all problems through fruitful discussions and dialogue, with counseling and with mutual prayer if we are inclined. If these steps are not happening in a significant relationship, then something or someone must give.

We can do our best to prevent such problems ahead of time. When you're a student and contemplating the rest of your life, please factor in your need to find a lifelong companion who will fully understand the requirements of your career choice and who will support you. And if your lifelong companion has a career, you must extend the same understanding and support.

These are competitive times, and succeeding is difficult even if we already have all our ducks in a row. It becomes even more difficult for anyone who has constant spats about work and career.

So please plan wisely and choose wisely. Factor all the information into your personal equation, and do so as soon as you can. This might well save you from lots and lots of heartache later on.

97 Give yourself the gift of longevity in your career!

Good things happen to you when you're able to stay in business for a prolonged time. First, the concept of momentum begins to come into play. Your word-of-mouth referrals grow each year, and you will also benefit when former clients come back again and again to you.

For example, Tom's firm has been in business for more than 20 years. Recently, he contacted a former client who'd given him a lot of business in the early years. Tom pitched a new idea to him, and it resulted in another successful project! Make sure to stay in contact with your former clients, so they'll know how to reach you. If you've delivered superior service to them in the past, they'll reward you with their loyalty today and in the future.

Not only that, but the mere fact that you've been engaged in the same enterprise for a long period says something about your success. You're still flourishing and delivering for your clients, while unsuccessful salespeople have had to move on to other endeavors.

Also, if your company provides a substantial benefits package, longevity is vital because the benefits accumulate at set yearly milestones. If things work out in your career, it will pay you to stay where you are so you can maximize the benefits that will provide for your retirement years.

98 Stay hungry!

One way to assure longevity in your sales career is to keep your edge by staying "lean and mean." We all start out hungry, but some of us start to become a little complacent when we experience tremendous success. There's always a danger of starting to believe that the sales will just keep coming and we can put our careers on "cruise control."

Keep that edge, and keep your work ethic at a high intensity level at all times – especially when you experience tremendous sales growth. As we've said earlier, that's actually the best time to attempt to turn up the work volume, because you'll feel a surge of confidence in your abilities.

When I was starting out, a good friend gave me some great advice: "Work hard to become successful – and then work harder, because it'll be even more difficult to handle that success!"

I can't tell you how many times I've seen successful, confident sales professionals lose it all overnight. So stay focused on your goals, and keep easing them ever higher as you progress. Stay current and motivated by attending workshops and seminars in your industry. Stay grounded as you earn more and more money.

When Tom was coaching youth football a few years ago, his young players would each put on a little show in the end zone after scoring a touchdown. After their first victory, Tom gathered his players in a huddle and suggested to them, "Act as if you've been there before."

This is good advice for all of us. So, stay hungry! And when you experience success, keep your focus on staying on top of your game.

99 | Keep practicing the fundamentals.

At every stage of our careers, we need to stay focused on the fundamentals of our businesses. To make the case for staying fundamentally sound in the business world, Tom cites analogies from professional sports. For instance, even though the strategies for both offense and defense in pro football become more and more sophisticated all the time, the outcome of actual games often comes down to execution of the fundamentals: Usually, the team that makes the fewest turnovers (loses the ball to the other team the least) wins the game.

Major League Baseball offers another example. In the spring training that precedes each season, the managers and coaches always have the players, even the most experienced, practice the fundamentals of the game. Just as the rookie hopefuls do, the returning veterans focus on the proper way to run the bases or lay down an important bunt. They rehearse the plays and relearn the rules in a controlled setting so they can win with fundamentally sound baseball all season.

We've given you these 100 points so you can focus on them and apply them where appropriate. If you do this, you'll be on your way to a successful career. What does this include?

1 Learn everything you can about your product or service.
2 Communicate each and every relevant sales benefit to your prospective clients and make a complete case for using you and your firm.
3 Roll up your sleeves and put in the hours that are required to find clients who can use your services and who actually will make transactions happen.
4 Provide these clients with superior service throughout the entire transaction.
5 Stay in touch with clients and find new and creative ways to reach new and better clients.
6 Conduct yourself in an honorable and distinguished manner throughout your career.
7 Stay hungry and stay current in your practice while protecting your niche as an expert in a given area of your industry.

100 Your biggest sale!

In the final analysis, you are the first person you have to close. How many of us have lingering doubts about our capabilities and our prospects for success in this competitive world? Sometimes it might be difficult for us to truly believe in ourselves, because of baggage we carry or external factors, or people, that have been a source of discouragement. But you can succeed!

Congratulations on completing these focus points! Now, here is some future homework for you. You've finished this book. Now, go back and read each of the focus points again. But this time, make notes in a writing tablet, using examples to illustrate the points, wherever possible from your own life or the lives of others whom you know. Just the act of writing something down improves the level of retention, and you need to truly focus your attention on these points.

If you accomplish this, you'll already be ahead of the game, because you'll be aware of many fundamental lessons that affect our success in our business careers. This fact will give you one more legitimate reason to truly begin to believe in your power to succeed.

Finally, take one more moment and think back to a point in time when you really felt as if you "had it together" in your life. It might be a time in high school or college when you were doing well. It might be a time when you were competing in a sport and you succeeded.

Think about how good you felt then and how you just knew you had what it took to get the results you desired. That's how we want you to feel again! We want you to be able to hit your prime, have the courage to determine your true objectives and then take the action steps required to make your objectives a reality!

Now it's on to "Sales 101" where we'll examine the sales process and deal with buyers' objections so we can close as many sales as possible in the future.

"Sales 101"

Sales skills have never been more important. Let's roll up our sleeves and take a closer look at how selling works.

I'm going to focus on the common denominators that exist in many different industries. Again, we're going to build from the ground up so we can create a foundation for you. Along the way, I'll encourage you to apply the principles until they become second nature in your daily sales regimen.

Right at the outset, I want you to know that it's critically important for you to focus on improving your sales skills. That's because even a small improvement in some of the following areas can dramatically increase your results in terms of sales and creating valuable business development relationships. These sales skills primarily involve four areas: Prospecting for clients, making persuasive sales presentations, overcoming your client's objections and closing your sales.

Briefly, let's get an overview of the entire sales process from start to finish. Here's the typical sales cycle:

1 Identify the target you want to reach
2 Do your homework and research to determine the best ways to reach the target
3 Create your sales script to use both in person and when leaving voice mail messages
4 Make the call
5 Get an initial client visit
6 Prepare for the initial client visit
7 Make your best presentation/impression at the initial client visit
8 Close your prospect
9 Follow up during and after the transaction
10 If everything has gone according to plan, seek referrals from this satisfied client

Before we even begin this sales process, we need to have a thorough working knowledge of the product or service we provide to our clients. In many industries, what we sell is our expertise in a given area. In a legal setting, a new client may come to us seeking preliminary advice about an imminent transaction. There might be legal concerns and many issues that have financial implications. For example, our client could desire to minimize any tax repercussions and maximize profit from the transaction. We'd better be able to help our client achieve this objective, so we need to know every step necessary to do that with maximum efficiency.

As you recall, when we began discussing our 100 behavioral focus points, we suggested that you start from "Day One" with a thirst for the knowledge of your industry. There will be a learning curve, and it will be difficult at first for every newcomer.

We've also encouraged you, if you're a veteran sales professional, to make the effort to stay up-to-date by reading trade publications and journals and by attending the continuing education courses and seminars that each industry has.

In the beginning stages, it's far better for you to allow a little more time to really learn your craft. That way, right from the start you'll give your clients the best service possible. We must start building a track record of satisfied clients who'll want to refer us to others who need similar services.

Single practitioners in given industries need to be very attentive to their clients. Often, when their business is booming, their workload literally overwhelms them – and client matters get pushed back for weeks and weeks.

The result is predictable. The ignored clients are patient at first, but then they become frustrated and angry at the poor service they're receiving. Unfortunately, your knowledge of a particular area of the law or financial specialty isn't always enough if you don't give top-priority treatment to your clients' affairs.

It's always better to have an effective quality control system in place. Rather than allow client concerns to pile up as they come in, such a system prioritizes the concerns and rates them as well. That lets the practitioner attend to the most pressing and important matters (the "A" stack) first and assign lesser-value ratings to other matters that a junior associate or "spillover" colleague who's just getting started can handle.

When practitioners run that type of system effectively, they create satisfied clients who'll refer more business to them; and the firm can begin to grow substantially.

Unfortunately, overworked individuals often don't believe they have the time to attend business or industry seminars or workshops that teach time management and organizational skills. These individuals could find another means of dealing with this problem, such as hiring a skilled office administrator to run the office effectively.

Many resources are available to us: Books written for our industries, current seminars, conventions, conferences and other special events that address topics of interest. In addition, we'll want to find an experienced mentor or manager in our office who can counsel us when we have a question or concern about a sales relationship.

Perhaps we can find a silver lining from the above example of overworked practitioners: We're not the only ones who struggle to find the time to get all our work done efficiently. We have lots of company!

After we've developed a complete understanding of our product or service, we're ready to become fully engaged in the sales process.

Let's start with our first objective: Identifying our target prospects. How do we locate prospects and build a database of potential clients for our products and services?

Many resources are available. For example, if we're a vendor selling our services or products in the advertising industry, we could consult a master directory such as

"The Agency Red Book" or a trade publication's resources such as the Adweek Directories. If we wanted to conduct a marketing campaign to alert all advertising agencies of our products or services, we could rent or purchase a list of prospects and then choose the most appropriate or cost-effective means of reaching them, such as a direct mail program.

This is a pretty universal process for all sales applications. We can consult such directories or trade publications for leads. We can attend trade shows and bring back the show directories to identify the exhibitors or attendees they profile. We can go to our local library. We can do quick searches via the Internet (a good use of our surfing skills). We can rent or buy lists from mailing list companies. Depending upon our industry, we can simply answer the phones in our office to get new prospects who call about existing inventory that we're offering for sale.

So most of us can acquire empirical data on prospects' addresses (e-mail and street) and phone numbers. We need to roll up our sleeves at first and begin to build a database because it will become one of our most valuable possessions after a while.

Once we've identified our prospects, we must find the best way to communicate with them so they'll know who we are and how we can provide benefits to them through our unique products and services. Sales professionals usually divide prospects into two groups: Warm and cold. The warm prospects are people we already know – and, more importantly, they already know us. The cold prospects are those who we don't know.

Remember Tom's real estate newsletter? One section provided updates on the sons and daughters of homeowners in the community. Because most parents were interested in keeping Tom current on their children, he became someone they wanted to speak with, not just another real estate agent they wanted to get rid of on the phone.

Exercise One:

Write down 20 people whom you would consider to be warm prospects for your products or services.

You'll want to contact the prospects on your warm list in an appropriate way that doesn't offend them. Perhaps you can meet them for dinner or lunch and just discuss your business in a conversational manner they won't perceive as trying to sell them. With warm prospects, it's usually enough just to let them know what you're doing. A good friend will often initiate a referral or make a valuable suggestion without you having to suggest it. That's what I do when I can help one of my friends.

However, make sure that you communicate your wins and accomplishments to members of this group; they already have a vested interest in your future!

You can contact cold prospects in several ways. Call them. Send them a letter or presentation about one or more benefits you can provide for them; this is sometimes known as a "value proposition." Send them an e-mail or a postcard with a "hook" to appeal to them, such as a listing of current sales prices in their neighborhood.

If you call your cold prospects, be prepared for the following:

- To deal with the prospect's "gatekeeper"
- To deal with the prospect's voice mail messaging system
- To deal with the prospect if he or she actually answers the phone

I've obtained some of my best clients through my relationship with their gatekeeper. Rather than treat a gatekeeper as an obstacle, I focused on finding ways to establish goodwill. I realized that most good gatekeepers do have the best interests of their boss in mind, so I let them know how important it would be for me to provide my assistance. In essence, I sold the gatekeeper so I could get in the door to sell the boss.

However, not all gatekeepers will want much to do with you. So you might want to use some tricks, such as calling the prospect very early or very late, or during the gatekeeper's lunch hour. Remember the focus point about "good news"; if you really have something your prospect will want to know about, use this one – it works!

As we know, voice mail is a fact of life today. Many key executives in large firms don't have a huge support staff anymore, so instead of dealing with a gatekeeper you might have to deal with a recording from the prospect. Contrary to what some salespeople think, leaving a voice mail message does not constitute building a relationship with the prospect; you still need to speak to a human being.

We all know the problems of voice mail and e-mail messages. Callbacks from your prospects are rare, and they might treat your message as unwanted spam. Here are a few tips:

1 Call often, and be creative about when you call. If you leave a message, make sure it is scripted (but doesn't sound like it), and make sure it presents a value proposition (the benefits) for the prospect. Your messages should be compelling, concise and brief. You're making your first impression with the client, so your English usage needs to be perfect! Practice your script often, so it sounds as real and compelling as possible. Limit your message to 30 seconds. Make sure you describe yourself and your company, plus the special value/benefit you can offer your prospect. Leave your phone number clearly and without rushing it – and you might want to repeat it once.

2 If you reach your prospect, deliver the script you've developed, but make sure you speak in more of a conversational manner, although still concisely. Finish up with an open-ended question. The purpose of this type of question is to prevent the prospect from dismissing you with a yes/no answer. Here are some examples:

Example 1: "I'll get my presentation to you by next Wednesday. When would be a good time for us to get together after you've had a chance to review the information?"

Example 2: "I really appreciate your spending time on the phone with me today. When would be a good time for me to follow up with you on this project?"

Example 3: (Alternative dates) "You sound really busy today, and I'd like to get you what you need immediately. Is next Tuesday or Wednesday better for you?"

Exercise Two:

Write a 30-second script to leave as a voice mail message, and a 30-second script to deliver when you reach your prospect.

Exercise Three:

Write three open-ended questions that you can use with your prospects.

Once we start to actually make contact with our prospects, we need to be prepared to sell! You might find it helpful to use role-playing sales games with your fellow sales associates to sharpen the sales skills you'll need when going face-to-face with your prospects. This is extremely beneficial, because it forces you to think on your feet and become more familiar with your benefits and communication skills.

Now we'll take a closer look at the features and benefits of what we sell. Let's say we're selling real estate in a community where we've been raised. Let's take a look at this fact from the feature/benefit standpoint.

Feature:
I live in this community and was raised here

Benefits:

- Commonality with other residents who have shared history in this community
- Knowledge and familiarity with community that can only come from living there for a long time
- Likelihood of establishing more trust with the other local residents (buyers and sellers) based upon your history (and your family's or firm's history in the community)

Now let's apply the same approach to the bigger/smaller firm examples.

Feature:
This firm is one of the largest in the industry

Benefits:

- Can bring more resources to bear for clients
- Volume of business results in savings to clients
- More transactions equal more experience and more expertise
- More transactions equal more business opportunities for clients
- Credibility and stature result from dealing with one of the largest firms

Feature:
This is a hungry, smaller-sized firm

Benefits:

- We really appreciate your business, and we'll provide you with the highest degree of service. Your business means more to us than it does to the bigger firm

- You won't get lost in the shuffle because we were too big to truly care about you
- We are experts at what you need, because our senior partner used to be with the large firm until we hired him. You get the benefits of expertise and customized service
- Our fees are more reasonable and affordable
- We can respond faster to your needs because we don't have a bureaucracy to deal with here

Exercise Four:

Write down the primary features of your product, service or firm; and create a list of at least three benefits for your prospects.

As you'll see, there are many ways you can "spin off" benefits from the features you're working with in your industry. Always quantify the benefits for your prospects, in terms of the economic value the benefits represent to them. But remember that your legal department or advisor will ask you to be careful about what you promise your prospects from this standpoint. So make sure you clear your specific pitch with your management.

Also, know when to move on to the next prospect if your chances of success with a given prospect are too small. No matter how attractive your benefits may be, if your prospect has a brother, other close relative or best friend currently handling the business, you'll want to move on to someone who will buy from you.

In this stage of the sales process, many of us can "psych ourselves out" if we're new to our industry or we lack a little self-confidence. But take heart – if you've approached your career properly, done all your home-work and research and have prepared for "doing battle" face-to-face with your prospects, you'll be ready, willing and able to make your first all-important sales.

When times get stressful - and they do for all of us – keep these affirmations handy so you can start to truly believe them:

- Your prospects want your product or service
- Your prospects need your product or service
- Your product or service is the latest (state of the art), biggest (most deluxe) or smallest (most compact); and your prospect just has to buy it now
- Your prospects are just waiting for you to call so they can place orders

The point of thinking positive thoughts such as these is simply to bolster your confidence. There is plenty of negativity around us. We do need to stay up if we're to succeed today.

Obviously, the affirmations above are just examples. You can create ones of your own if they're more in tune with your situation.

Also, it's important for us to understand some of the pri-mary reasons that prospects don't buy our product or service. Here are my "Top Ten" reasons:

1. Your product or service is not the best (or is not available at competitive rates)
2. Your product or service does not stand out (or is unknown to the prospect)
3. Your prospect keeps procrastinating or coming up with excuses or objections
4. Your prospect doesn't want to "pay the piper" and spend the money for your product or service
5. Your prospect is happy with his or her current supplier (this prospect might be a good future prospect for you, however, because of this loyalty factor)
6. Your prospect doesn't trust you or your firm
7. Your prospect has had a bad past experience that is affecting his decision-making
8. Your prospect is indecisive (remember Focus Point #46)
9. Your timing is poor for this sale
10. You never asked for the prospect's business

Exercise Five:

List your own "Top Ten" reasons for losing any sales or opportunities to sell in the past year. Consider what you could've done to improve the outcome.

Now we're going to discuss the initial client meeting. Remember the saying, "You only have one chance to make a good first impression," because it is true. So let's review what we need to do to assure our success in meeting our prospect.

Try to learn as much as you can about what your prospect needs in your telephone and e-mail communications. If you get some good insights, make sure you do your research so you can state your case effectively when you meet with the client.

If you're unable to get much insight from your prospect, the other sources we've mentioned will help you find out more about the prospect's current production levels. It's always advantageous to learn as much as possible about a client's preferences before you meet, so you can bring presentation materials and "leave-behinds" that specifically address the prospect's concerns.

When your initial meeting is a "one-on-one" between you and your prospect, make your arrangements, schedule the meeting time and just show up at that time. Do not call on the morning of the scheduled appointment to confirm.

If you call in advance, you're giving the prospect a chance to postpone or cancel the meeting. Because the meeting has been set for the prospect's office, the prospect will probably be there even if he or she has forgotten about the appointment. If your prospect has left for another luncheon engagement or meeting, he or she now owes you big-time; and you can always set another time when you get back in touch with your prospect.

My experience has been completely positive with this technique; 99% of the time, the prospect is waiting for our initial meeting without any prompt. That's the bottom line.

Naturally, though, if the meeting will involve more than just two individuals – especially if your boss will be there – you'll want to call to confirm on the morning of the meeting. In this case, the downside is too great for you.

You will be blamed for any misunderstandings or confusion about the meeting.

Do you remember our discussion about features and benefits? When you meet your client for the first time, you want to make your case with the most relevant and persuasive benefits that flow from the features of your product or service. And it's really important for you to learn about their business by asking them probing questions.

Depending upon your objectives for this initial meeting, you might be able to dispel any misconceptions your prospect might have about your product or service. You might be able to overcome your prospect's objections, too. And if you really get lucky, you might even have a chance to close the prospect and bring home the business!

In time, you'll gain valuable instinct and perspective for dealing with prospects. You'll learn how to read them. You'll become experienced at ascertaining the nuances of prospects' characters and personalities in just one meeting at their office. And with a little seasoning, you'll just know when to go for the close.

Obviously, you'll apply all the focus points about your appearance and the need for appropriate attire. You'll also need to be sensitive to your surroundings when you meet your prospect. You'll have a lot on your mind concerning the prospect's expressed needs, but you'll also want to pay close attention to the environment and social interaction you observe. Pay attention to your prospect so you can get the best idea of how to approach him or her at this meeting and in the future.

You'll want to arrive at least 10 minutes early, so please take into account the specific traffic congestion in the area and on your route there. And if you live in Southern California, you should multiply that figure of 10 minutes by three!

Whenever we meet our prospective clients, we always want to have clear objectives in mind. Here are a few of my favorites:

1 Learn as much as possible about prospects and their needs. That way, you can return with a proposal that meets those needs and gets you the business.
2 If you've received in-depth understanding of your prospect's needs in a preliminary communication, fill your proposal with as many effective benefits as you can. Also, if the prospect expressed any preliminary objections in your earlier discussion, overcome them and set the stage, in your proposal, for your close.
3 Use the initial client meeting to set the stage for your second appointment. In this case, your primary goal is relationship building so you can take things to the next level and prepare your prospect for a later close.
4 Use the initial meeting as a forum where you can establish your credentials. Then, when the prospect does have an appropriate project in the offing, your firm will be a viable option for that project.
5 One of your most important objectives is always to meet on a face-to-face basis. You'll find that your personality is a good fit with some of your prospects. Perhaps you share an interest in an activity such as golf or long distance running. This is also another area where it pays to have done your homework.

Perhaps your prospect was featured in a trade publication interview or has been at the forefront of a vital local community issue. If there is any information out there on this prospect, you need to know about it. Make reviewing your prospect's web site part of your standard operating procedure in preparing for your initial client meeting! If you can find a way to bond or form a beginning relationship with this prospect, you've gotten that foot of yours in the door!

Just as we use open-ended questions to elicit the responses we want from our prospects, we'll want to find reasons for a follow-up meeting. For example, if the client expresses a reservation that we can address at a subsequent time, we can make a mental note to conclude the meeting by restating the prospect's concern and promising to address it in a meaningful way in your next meeting.

Many veteran sales professionals view the ability to overcome the objections of the prospect, and to close, as the hallmarks of a fundamentally sound salesperson. In fact, in some cyclical professions such as real estate, which can go from hot to cold very quickly, seasoned pros often have disdain for the inexperienced salesperson who hasn't mastered these skills. The pros call these rookies "order takers" and not salespersons. Having experienced these challenges in my own sales career, I will just say that you won't become a true sales professional until you learn how to overcome objections!

The brutal facts often bear out this assessment. When a bear market sets in, many sales agents begin to disappear from the sales landscape. So let's find out more about the art of overcoming our prospect's objections.

Let's take a look at some common objections:

1 Your prices are too high or your fees are too expensive
2 I'm happy with my current vendor/supplier
3 I don't have time to talk with you
4 I had a bad experience with your firm before
5 This idea is too risky for me
6 I haven't heard of you and I only work with the best firms
7 Your firm is too large for my needs
8 Your firm is too small for my needs
9 Your location is not convenient for me
10 I'm not that impressed with your product or service

Here's why you are hearing the above objections:

Objection #1:
"Your prices are too high or your fees are too expensive."

This means you haven't completely convinced your prospect of the value of your product or service. You need to establish the benefits the prospect will receive from your firm's expert advice or counsel. Your prospect's focus needs to be on the big picture and the total savings that are possible as a result of receiving the best services possible.

Objection #2:
"I'm happy with my current vendor."

Unless you have a powerful antidote that overcomes this satisfaction (such as a benefit that is overwhelming for the prospect's situation), the best approach is to acknowledge the prospect's answer and attempt to find out more information about his or her specific needs. When I encounter prospects who support their current supplier, I focus on a long-term approach that might earn me a piece of the business down the road. These prospects usually become good clients if you stay in the picture with them and build a relationship that will let you pitch a portion of their business at a later time.

Objection #3:
"I don't have time to talk with you."

If you get a quick brush-off, use an open-ended question to get permission to call back at a better time. Also, when you do get the chance to talk to them, you'll need to offer a value proposition about your product or service to get their interest. This is a fancy way of saying that you need to find a "hook" or idea that will get their attention. For example, if you sold the home next door to them, that would interest them.

Objection #4:
"I had a bad experience with your firm before."

This type of objection can work to your advantage if it's an honest one. Taking the time to listen to your prospect's "beef" demonstrates that you care enough to make things right. This is actually a helpful stage in building a relationship with such a prospect. Also, this setting gives you the chance to point out any personnel and policy changes that have taken place since that "old business" occurred.

Objection #5:
"This idea is too risky for me."

If your prospective client still believes your approach is too risky, then you've failed to provide a convincing argument for the value of your product or service. Another approach with prospects who are either extremely timid or really "old school" is to invite them to bring trusted advisors or family members to your next meeting. But once that meeting is set, make sure you have your complete arsenal of relevant and compelling benefits ready so you can address your prospect's specific needs.

Objection #6:
"I haven't heard of you, and I only work with the best firms."

Again, provide this prospect with a value proposition to overcome this barrier. For example, if you've just performed your services for a current client with similar needs, tell this prospect about that. If your service is the best in your field, get your prospect's attention by mentioning the good results you've gotten for other clients.

For more ammunition, ask your happy current clients to provide testimonials for you and then include them in your promotional materials and leave-behinds.

Exercise Six:

Create your own responses for the remaining four objections. Refer to the earlier section on features and benefits that addresses big firm and small firm benefits.

Now let's move on to closing techniques.

For me, closing has always been the fun part of the sales process. After all, this is the moment when it all comes together for you. Your prospect's needs and the product or service that you're selling or offering become one – and the deal is done!

Really, we're always in some stage of closing our clients and prospects. My goal is to move the sales process along from one step to the next. Each time I'm successful at this, I know my chances are that much better that I will get the business I'm seeking. I actually think of such steps as "small closes" that lead to the big one.

One of the most important factors in knowing when to advance to the next step is the feedback you receive from your prospect. As you become more experienced, you'll be able to read your prospects and the signals they're sending you. Obviously, when we first engage our prospects, they're not yet interested in what we can do for them. As we get to know them and, more importantly, as we become aware of their needs, we can build their interest in what we can provide them.

Our challenge is to advance through the sales process with them and accurately gauge when they're ready to make the next step. As we've learned, we must make the best first impression possible with each prospect. Next, we must find a way to engage them appropriately, such as a referral or a marketing contact, which could include direct mail, the telephone (either in person or via voice mail) or an e-mail at first. Next, we get that initial meeting and we try to learn all we can about their needs and their ability to buy our product or service.

Some veteran sales pros like to refer to the later stages – overcoming objections and, ultimately, the close – as "the dance" with the prospect. That's because we're close to our goal of getting their business. As our prospects become more interested and start asking more questions that lead us to believe their threshold of interest is increasing, we need to be ready to make a smooth transition into the closing mode.

Sales professionals employ any number of closes. I'm going to deal with some of the most common and effective ones.

1 Basic Verbal Close. You're either face-to-face or speaking on the phone with your prospect and you guide the conversation to the point at which you think the prospect is ready to take the next step. The objective here is to keep moving your prospect down the path by eliminating any excuses or fears and by building the prospect's level of confidence in your product or service.

It's so interesting to me to learn of situations where sales professionals start out with nothing more than a cold call and end up with a closed prospect after a few minutes of conversation. We always like to improve our odds whenever possible, but there still are situations where timing is everything. When you're having one of those "months with the gods" when everything you touch turns into a large commission, your confidence and professionalism can just be contagious. Your prospects will sense that, and they'll want to work with you because of it!

2 Basic Written Close. Why not let your contracts and paperwork do your closing for you whenever possible? This next little piece of advice will elicit a smile from you if you happen to be a real estate salesperson or broker. Each and every time you meet with a prospect; always have a pen that works and the appropriate paperwork ready for your prospect to sign! While you're meeting with your prospect, you answer every one of the concerns, objections or questions in a satisfactory manner that lets you move to your smooth, written closing statement. At just the right time, you calmly mention that you did bring the necessary order form, offer form, agreement, etc. with you for the prospect's convenience. Next, you just reach for the order form and begin taking their information. It can be this simple!

3 Assumptive Close. When you're on one of those "hot" streaks and things are going your way, you'll even want to try this once in a while. The essence of this closing proposition is that you're confident your prospect is fully responding to your presentation and that your product or service is a great fit for them. You move this close along by acting as if the deal is going to happen. You can start by asking a specific question that relates to the order process at your prospect's firm. Depending upon how ready your prospect is, you can quickly move this entire close along to the signing stage.

However, be careful with this one, because it can backfire. The prospect can bolt if you've misread the signals. Often, problems with trusting can cause your prospect to delay the sales process and to interpret your assumptive close as unwanted pressure.

To avoid this negative outcome, you might want to ask a couple of hypothetical questions about the ordering process at your prospect's firm. By asking "what if" questions, it is less likely that your prospect will bolt and more likely that he or she will send you more accurate signals thereafter. If your prospect still wants to keep things on a more preliminary basis, you'll hear the qualifications immediately after your "what if" questions. If you do receive this "two steps forward, one step back" response, at least you know you have more work to do with the prospect.

But if all of the signals are green lights, just go with the flow! You could even pose an open-ended question such as, "When do you want to take delivery on this order – next Wednesday or next Friday?"

4 Sharp Angle Close. When your prospect or client responds to your sales initiatives by throwing down the gauntlet with a condition or two that you need to do to get this sale, take a look at what's being proposed. If the prospect's request is reasonable, you've just made yourself a sale.

However, as you can imagine, this closing response can be tricky. If your prospect is looking for substantial concessions that really eliminate most of the profit your firm is to receive, you've got a problem. Just be careful when this challenge occurs with a new prospect, because you really don't know the person yet. If you lean too much on your management people, make sure it really is the right work for everyone at your firm. The worst possible scenario occurs when you do your part but the prospect turns out to be a bit flaky or even rather unscrupulous. Be careful out there and try not to get burned by a prospect or client who turns out to be exceedingly difficult.

5 Other Successful Closes. Often, we need to develop techniques that just seem to work for us. I've known some extremely successful "closers" who preferred to get their prospects on their turf, such as a golf course, country club or a coveted corporate suite for the hottest professional sports game in town.

Other "closers" use techniques that appear to flow from their personalities. They like to build the relationship by being there for the prospect with helpful information that is useful and that indicates expertise in their area of sales. One extremely successful real estate professional always did his closing in his expensive Mercedes. He drove an ultra-luxury model and spent most of his time driving prospects around to properties that he'd bought or sold for his clients. After 30 minutes, "Ted" had set the stage for his close back at his office in Beverly Hills. I guess if you've got it, flaunt it!

Whatever works for you, just do it when the time is right. Unfortunately, I've known salespersons who never asked for the order. Yes, they spent time with their prospects, but they never got around to the close! In my practice, we pay special attention to mastering vital sales techniques that we need to overcome objections and to close our deals.

The successful close will set the stage for you and your firm to deliver on your promises. It will let you sell your product or perform your service in behalf of this new client. Stay in constant communication with your client and assist the client through every phase and element of the sales transaction. That way, there are no negative surprises, and any contingencies can be worked out in the best possible way.

Your ability to deliver will turn your client into a happy one who'll be delighted to refer you to others who need your product or service as well. Remember the example of the pyramid of "word of mouth" clients that we want to build in our practice? That pyramid is built on the satisfaction of our previous and current clients. We want clients who will tell others, "I've got an amazing real estate broker. You've got to give him a call."

No one masters this entire process overnight. But if you do decide to make the effort, you can accomplish pretty amazing results in sales-related industries.

If all this seems a little daunting, don't worry. Our enterprises are important, but we're not dealing with life and death matters here. If we have a bad day, we lose a sale or a prospect – but let's keep our perspective about the whole endeavor.

So while we urge you to give this important work your full attention, we also encourage you to take a deep breath and relax from time to time. This is not brain surgery! Selling becomes satisfying and fun when you maintain your positive attitude, know your area of expertise and deliver on your word.

Keep your sense of humor in play so you can enjoy each day. Find the proper balance that allows you to succeed at the highest level but to continue to enjoy the gift of life that we all possess. Maintain your balance and make an effort to keep this whole process in perspective. Then you'll be improving your odds of succeeding over the entire course that we run throughout our business careers.

Now that we've had this crash course on the sales process from the beginning of the transaction to the conclusion, we're going to consider a couple of more long-term approaches in the next chapter.

"Long-Term Relationships and Networking"

Remember when we discussed the need to take the long view in building a successful career in your industry? We spoke of the need to approach our competitive avenues much like a marathon runner would, not a sprinter. We will build our lasting success in our industries and communities on the strong foundation of sound relationships with those around us. Your sales success will be determined over the long haul by the quality of the relationships you maintain with your clients and your network of influence.

For many of us, our relationships come first when it is time to make a purchase or an acquisition. We think about the people we know and trust, and then we make the call. That's the way it is, especially in today's complicated business world.

Virtually all the relationship-selling models employed today gauge basic human behavior similarly, and consistent with the above example.

The initial and most important requirement is to establish trust in the relationship. Next, we need to assess the prospect's true needs and begin to provide satisfying solutions that meet those needs. Finally, it all comes together for the sale and for our relationship when we close our prospect and unite his or her needs with our product or services.

When you think about it, this is one of those areas that many of us should already feel pretty good about. Most of us have formed a number of productive relationships throughout our lives. This is something that we all know something about. The challenge for us is to increase our spheres of influence and to reach more and more new prospects.

The following frequently asked questions will help simplify this process for us.

Question:
When should we begin the relationship stage with our prospects?

Answer:
As early as possible while you still have reasons to visit or stay in contact with your prospect.

Question:
What beginning steps can we take to help this bonding process along?

Answer:
First, demonstrate your interest in your prospect by asking intelligent and thorough questions. They'll help you

understand all the implications involved in your prospect's needs. Once you've gained these insights, you'll be on your way to finding the right solutions for the prospect. As we've discussed, we should also always be aware of the need to continually progress to the next step in the sales cycle so we're moving this relationship closer and closer to the final close and the sale that we'll have earned.

Question:
What happens to this relationship when the prospect becomes our new client?

Answer:
We'll need to accelerate the relationship by providing our products or services in the best context possible. We'll want to make sure that our work is superior and that all our communications with our new client are clear and completely understood. Clients need to know that we have their best interests at heart. We need to maintain frequent contact and stay available to them. We must be prepared to handle all of our client's concerns throughout the entire duration of our business together.

In the early stages of our relationship it is critical that we plan our time well so we can personally supervise the most important stages and events that take place on behalf of this new client. For example, in the printing industry the press run is a major event for the client and the printing firm. As this relationship matures, we'll be able to introduce more of a team approach to selling our existing accounts – but we must always ensure that our clients' interests are in trusted hands.

Question:
Once we identify a new prospect as a priority lead, what types of steps will bring this prospect into our individual or firm fold?

Answer:
We'll want to communicate to our prospects the high esteem in which we hold them. In every way, we'll want our new prospects to feel as if they're the most important persons in our business lives. So we'll treat them much like a college football coach would treat a "blue chip" high school recruit. We'll attend to them, ascertain their concerns and come up with solutions for them before we attempt to close them.

However, like many truly great athletic coaches, we'll maintain this relationship with these prized recruits for life! We'll want to ensure that their needs are met. We'll stay in touch with them and allow them to become an important part of our influence network after any transaction is completed. We must always remember that our relationships are for life, not just for the period in which we derive our financial gain. The truly successful sales professionals have vast numbers of satisfied customers who frequently refer them to new prospects and clients.

Question:
Is there a new client profile that we'll want to match?

Answer:
A number of considerations definitely should be at work in this process. We'll want to find prospects who are well into the development curve in their careers. We want

decision-makers who are clear about their objectives and who are talented and resourceful enough to become major players in their given fields.

In addition, we'll want to work with individuals who share our values with respect to providing the highest quality of services or products in the marketplace. This profile will ensure that prospects who do become new clients will influence others in a positive way that will benefit our practice by attracting other bright stars into our fold.

Finally, if our new clients' businesses are flourishing, it will be easier for us to actually get paid for all of the services and products that we provide to them!

By focusing on a given niche in an industry, you can actually increase your results in areas you want to focus on. If you're able to provide continual results for these highly valued clients who are also your good friends, you will have the opportunity to build a successful practice that achieves longevity – which is the ultimate goal, after all.

Now, let's look at what comprises a successful sales network.

We hear so much about networking these days. What is it, exactly? A network is simply a group of individuals who help each individual in the network get where he or she wants to go as quickly and efficiently as possible.

What are some of the benefits of having a strong network in place? Here is my short list of benefits, which provides you with the following:

1 Increased access to products and services
2 Additional moral support, and different points of view when you need more "takes" on a particular problem or situation
3 A multitude of qualified referrals for products and services
4 Introductions to new individuals
5 Increased opportunities to be of service to others
6 Fellowship and friendship opportunities
7 Additional opportunities for philanthropic involvement
8 More knowledge and access to more resources
9 Increased power in your business and personal life
10 Increased sense of confidence in your ability to assist others

Perhaps you can think of more benefits?

This is a good place for an action exercise. Take out a blank sheet of paper and draw a circle. Now place a small dot in the middle. Begin to draw lines from the dot in the middle to the outer edge of the circle. Keep adding new lines that are equidistant from that initial line until you have gone completely around the circumference of the circle.

You now have a rough image of your network. Just like a bicycle wheel or other powerful form of transportation, you've created a dynamic wheel of influence that can take you where you want to go. Write the names of your fellow associates just outside the intersection of the lines and the outer edge of the circle. Imagine a time when you might be able to list scores of network associates who'll play a positive role in your individual and collective success.

This is where we want to go.

Here are a few more frequently asked questions about networking:

Question:
How often do we work on our networks?

Answer:
This should be an activity that you are engaged in relentlessly on a "24x7" basis. For example, if you are in sales, whenever you are in a public place (such as a restaurant, office building, coffee shop or department store), you should allow yourself to be available to interact with a fellow human being in a natural manner.

Always make eye contact with others and smile so they'll know you're approachable in this setting. If you notice something about the person who is sitting next to you, this can be the basis for a polite remark or quip. That can often spark a fruitful discussion that will lead you directly or indirectly to someone who can avail themselves of your services. It takes an effort to reach out to others, and sometimes we need to start in small ways. But the important thing is to make that effort!

There are always exceptions to every bit of advice. Obviously, if you live in a major metropolis where people just don't communicate with individuals they don't already know, or if you don't feel comfortable in your immediate environment, you can continue to read your newspaper or book in complete anonymity. However, if you knew how many great sales leads were developed in natural settings such as the local Starbucks store,you just might become a little more "friendly" in such circumstances!

Question:
What are some of the best places to network in our industries?

Answer:
Some of the best places are trade conventions and seminars that address specific niche concerns and trends. The great thing about the trade convention is that everyone is in one place for a set duration, and we can find a way to interact with most of the key players in a quality way. Make sure to keep the focus on just making contact with these individuals in a quality manner. Go easy on the sales talk in this setting. You'll just want to make contact and get to know these individuals personally, and then you can meet some of their friends as well.

Question:
What type of behavior is accepted at such functions?

Answer:
As we mentioned, we want to avoid the "hard sell" here. And we'll want to limit our promotional efforts to responding quickly to queries about our practices. Also, it is usually all right to either ask for a business card or to give your card to someone else. However, it's best if you don't foist your card onto others; wait until they ask you for it. Also, practice a brief description that you can provide about your business.

Question:
What are some of the things to avoid in this type of setting?

Answer:
Be careful not to get trapped in prolonged discussions with people who will monopolize you because they don't know anyone either. At a reception, you can always leave by heading off to the bar for another diet cola or a drink for someone you know.

Question:
What are some things you can do to help yourself in this setting?

Answer:
The key in such circumstances is to be polite and graceful with everyone you meet, but to keep circulating as well. Many people there can do you a lot of good! The best strategy is to attend such events in the company of someone whom many attendees know and admire. This will ensure that your initial introduction (and first impression) is favorable because you're already in the presence of a respected opinion leader.

When the sales conference concludes, find a good time and place to review each and every business card that you have received. Transcribe relevant data into your data bank. This "debriefing" is invaluable. We need to make sure that we log all information while our conversations are fresh in our memory.

Also, if we offered to make inquiries or perform service for anyone we met, we'll want to follow through on those commitments as soon as possible when we return to our office.

When considering who could or should be a part of your network, look to your community, your industry and beyond. Sometimes, a connected and dynamic individual from another industry can bring you a great deal of new business. Because some attorneys specialize in one or two rather well defined areas of the law, it might be valuable for them to meet other lawyers who work in other categories and areas. In addition, many attorneys belong to country clubs, legal service organizations, alumni organizations, non-profit organizations and other community groups.

Now it's time for another action exercise. Write down the names of your current network professionals. This list could include leading business executives, attorneys, certified public accountants, business management analysts and consultants, and media executives such as the editor of your local newspaper or the CEO or senior management of the local television or radio station, etc.

Now write down the names (or an affiliation that will describe the network professional) of such individuals in your community whom you could add to your network. What would it mean for your practice to be able to receive referrals from some of the leaders of your community or industry? Obviously, this would be invaluable for you on every level.

If you don't have such a network today, resolve to make substantial progress in this area in the weeks ahead. My "coaching homework" for you is to first identify people you want to get to know and then take tangible steps toward making that a reality.

By the way, some communities have leadership programs in place to organize regular seminars for members. Tom has attended "Leadership Long Beach" seminars; he finds them to be an exceptional civic organization that challenges participants to seek excellence in their approach to their work careers and their community activities.

In addition, when you're meeting a potential network prospect for the first time, focus on developing the relationship first so things can progress in a relaxed manner. After a while, your prospect will be quizzing you on your areas of expertise and a natural bond can be formed. In these settings, always remember to include benefits for the "other guy" to receive from such an alliance.

So what have we learned in this chapter?

We've again emphasized our need to think long-term in our work career. We've acknowledged the vital role that good relationships play in our career achievements. I've included some frequently asked questions, and my answers to them involve both relationship building and networking. Finally, we've encouraged you to begin to take tangible steps to build your own network if one is not already in place.

Now it's on to Chapter Eight for some final thoughts.

"You've Got to Want It"

As we said in the beginning of this book, successful sales professionals display many characteristics. We mentioned the four elements of *momentum, consistency, patience* and *perseverance.* We also stated the importance of staying *balanced* in all vital dimensions of our lives.

We've provided 100 focus points relating to suggested behavior, sales practices and career longevity. Most of our focus points suggest things you should do. However, there are also many examples of negatives to avoid.

We've discussed different excuses that can come into play, as well as negative practices such as wasting your time surfing the Internet when you should be working for your company or employer. So why would anyone behave this way?

Human beings are not perfect; we all have our shortcomings. If you're attempting to change a negative behavior that's wasting your valuable time or resources, why not adopt the approach we suggested in Chapter One: Instead of trying to go from "A-to-Z" overnight, just focus on going from "A-to-B" first!

A good "A-to-B" step is to avoid the negative behavior for one day and then to go one more day after that. This way, your task won't seem daunting – and you'll increase your chances for success.

Let's be honest. It takes an extremely strong individual to succeed as a sales professional in most of our industries. There will be times when you experience rejection of your sales overtures. You need to be unfazed by such temporary setbacks. And if you do manage to succeed over an extended period of time, you'll still encounter challenges such as downturns in the economy and pressure from competitors.

You need to prepare for times when things get difficult (and they will). Expect to run into people who challenge your patience. Others might even try to undermine your success if they think that it is in their interest. Fortunately, such people usually undermine their own careers; but you might have to deal with the frustration until they're gone.

Times such as those help prove the value of having loyal friends and family supporters in your camp when it counts. Also, if you've "been there" for others in their struggles, you'll have friends for times when you're struggling!

If you've followed our advice about the steps you need to take to establish a strong foundation, you will be ready for a successful launch once you're at the threshold with your first few prospects and clients.

Because of the "up and down" nature of sales, it will be essential to find ways to maintain a high level of enthusiasm – especially when meeting prospects and clients and relating to them. It helps some salespeople to think of themselves as performers on stage and their prospects and clients as their audience. We all know how important it is for performers to be at their best when they perform. Do your best to make sure you're always "on" when you have a potential prospect or client within reach.

Students in school have to follow regular procedures if they want to confirm their understanding of the material they need to learn. Most of us got used to the idea of doing our homework, such as reading assignments or answering questions about the material. Not only that, but at regular intervals we studied for the quizzes, midterms and final exams that would determine much of the grade for our classes.

The point is, if you took the time to really listen in class and to do the required reading and studying, you had confidence before you sat down to take your exams. In a way, you already knew you'd do well.

This is the same approach we suggest in the real-world "exam" of sales and selling. Do everything you can to make these tasks more enjoyable, but do them.

In the final analysis: If we take the time to really learn our craft, our products and our services, and if we focus our efforts productively and over a sustained period, we will be successful! And once you experience this initial success, it should fuel your desire for even more success.

When you look at "Leslie's Library" in the back of this book, you'll see valuable references to some of the masters in sales. These works have all played a role in my success. I encourage you to make an investment in your own sales and motivational library. If a particular motion picture or book works for you, keep coming back to it. Tom has seen the high school basketball underdog movie "Hoosiers" about 20 times, and he immensely enjoys the film "Miracle," based on the true story of the USA Men's Hockey Team that overcame the odds to win an Olympic gold medal in Lake Placid in 1980.

Use all these resources and more to keep your desire intact so you can keep performing in your sales arena each and every day, week, month and year. When you can sustain a consistent level of outstanding results over time, you will succeed. Then it will merely be a matter of how successful you'll be.

In my coaching practice, I've encountered individuals who've gotten stuck in an unproductive mode that affects everything they do while they're frozen in place. How could this happen? Usually some event outside of their control will occur that is frustrating for them and they become fixated on it.

For example, perhaps they're awaiting the outcome of a sales presentation they've made. Assuming that everything was provided to the decision-maker, there's nothing left to do in this situation but wait until the outcome is revealed.

This is an example of a situation where you have no control over the outcome. When we find that this is the case, we must just mentally place this matter on the shelf and move on to the next task at hand. When we focus our attention on a situation or person that is beyond our control, we're wasting our time.

Sometimes, we have indirect control over a situation that is frustrating for us. Say that the traffic is a nightmare where you live (Southern California, anyone?). You do have some degree of control. You could leave an hour or more early or find a more efficient route to get you where you need to go. In this setting, you do have some options.

Can you think of something that is totally within your control? One thing that you control is your reactions and responses to challenging circumstances. When you encounter adversity, you have the power to turn a negative around and create an opportunity for your success. The more you engage in this type of positive thinking, the stronger you will become. It's amazing how much power each one of us has to make decisions in life that will help us to succeed or will sabotage our potential to succeed.

Let's look at a few simple choices we can make:

- To keep a positive frame of mind at all times. If something happens that challenges us, we can refuse to let it defeat us
- To become more patient when confronting difficult or frustrating circumstances
- To create our plans so we'll have our road map for success
- To follow up with the action steps required to get where we want to go
- To keep track of our time and monitor it so we know what our return on this investment really is

- To keep our goals in mind and maintain a maximum level of commitment and desire at all times
- To stay focused on what we can control in this life
- To maintain constant commitment to learning and improving the quality of the services we provide
- To build lasting relationships and networks that will help us achieve longevity in our fields
- To spend face-to-face time with our clients and provide them with the highest possible degree of service

Conversely, we never want to:

- Cancel a first meeting with a prospect or client
- Argue with a prospect or client
- Forget who's paying the bills, either in our office or in our practice
- Spread negative information about a rival, colleague or client
- Focus on price instead of the value we provide
- Quit defining our goals or believing in our dreams
- Stop listening
- Stop learning
- Stop showing up
- Stop trying

We've all seen those stirring moments on film when a coach gives an inspirational pep talk to his team just before the big game. Pretend for a moment that you are the coach. Whenever you are tempted to throw in the towel because things just don't seem to be working out the way you planned, take a brief "timeout" to consider:

- The time and energy you've already invested
- The funding that's been required for your learning curve
- The times in your life that you didn't let anything stand in your way because you were completely committed to doing something
- The satisfaction you're going to experience when you look back at this "defining moment" months or years from now
- How much fun you'll have after your next big transaction, when you give yourself that special reward you desire

In difficult times, it does seem to come down to that last word in the previous sentence: desire. Those classic expressions that we learned when we were playing sports still do apply. You do have to really want it, you know.

Tom enjoys speaking to students about career choices. When the students learn that he's been able to incorporate two of his passions, music and sports, into his life's work, someone always asks him what he would have done if things hadn't worked out.

His answer is always the same: "Failing was never an option. This was something I had to do." Remember Tom's 50 lunches and dinners with key executives from the sports and entertainment industry? He made his plan, and then he began taking his action steps to get to where he wanted to go. He wanted it – and he turned his dream into a reality.

So if we really do "have what it takes" and we put our whole heart into accomplishing our goal, who can stop us?

Now, on a different topic:

From time to time we all experience the numbing emotion we call fear. Some of us are afraid of making a mistake in front of our clients or bosses. Others have tremendous fears about such things as public speaking or being the center of attention in a large group.

Don't get down on yourself about fear. We're only human, and this is part of the human condition. When you find yourself in a fearful state, don't worry. Just confront it, and that will help you conquer it. You can keep moving forward in selling, and you will!

I want to close with a true story about my client "Susan," whom you met in Chapter Two. She's the client who wanted to remodel her kitchen so we reinforced her plan with visualization techniques that included a picture of a beautiful new kitchen posted in a prominent place where she sees it every day.

Susan has been a coaching client of mine for three years. If you ask, "Why so long?" the short answer is that she insists I keep working with her. Each year we've set ever-higher sales revenue goals and deeper levels of relationship building. The results continue to be exceptional, and Susan's sales revenues have increased 70% from that first year through the end of the third year.

Quite simply, although we started out with a one-year plan, Susan still believes that this coaching relationship keeps working for her, and that profits far exceed the cost. I could not be more proud of her commitment and work ethic. Susan bought in. She made the effort. And the result is that she has dramatically increased productivity and the return on her investment of time.

Susan is living proof of what awaits you when you truly decide to make a firm commitment to personal and professional growth. Then you will really be able to *Picture Yourself & the Life You Want!*

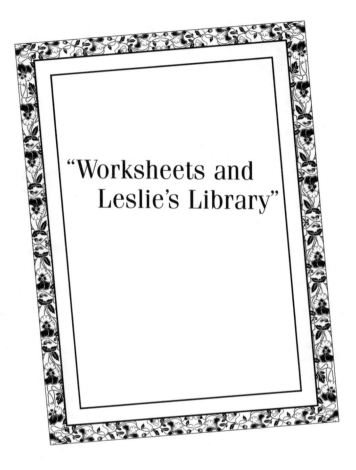

"Worksheets and
Leslie's Library"

Picture Yourself
& the Life
You Want

Open Ended Questions
Worksheet

Open

1 _____

2. _____

3. _____

4. _____

5. _____

6. _____

7. _____

8. _____

9. _____

10. _____

11. _____

12. _____

Picture Yourself
& the Life
You Want

Objections Worksheet

Objections	Reasonable Answer
1 _____	_____
2. _____	_____
3. _____	_____
4. _____	_____
5. _____	_____
6. _____	_____
7. _____	_____
8. _____	_____
9. _____	_____
10. _____	_____
11. _____	_____
12. _____	_____

Picture Yourself
& the Life
You Want

Feature and Benefit
Worksheet

Features   Benefits

1 _____   _____

2. _____   _____

3. _____   _____

4. _____   _____

5. _____   _____

6. _____   _____

7. _____   _____

8. _____   _____

9. _____   _____

10. _____   _____

11. _____   _____

12. _____   _____

Picture Yourself
& the Life
You Want

Warm Prospects
Worksheet

1. _____
2. _____
3. _____
4. _____
5. _____
6. _____
7. _____
8. _____
9. _____
10. _____
11. _____
12. _____
13. _____
14. _____
15. _____
16. _____
17. _____
18. _____
19. _____
20. _____

Picture Yourself
& the Life
You Want

Leslie's Library

Awaken The Giant Within
– Anthony Robbins

How To Master The Art of Selling
– Tom Hopkins

Who Moved My Cheese?
– Spencer Johnson, M.D.

Raving Fans
– Ken Blanchard & Sheldon Bowles

Advanced Selling Strategies
– Brian Tracy

How To Become A Rainmaker
– Jeffery Fox

The 7 Habits of Highly Effective People
– Stephen R. Covey

Risk, Originality & Virtuosity, the Keys to a Perfect 10
– Peter Vidmar